Show Up for Yourself

A GUIDE TO INNER GROWTH AND AWARENESS

Janet Philbin, LCSW, CHt

FINN-PHYLLIS
PRESS

Published by Finn-Phyllis Press, Inc.

Cover design by JetLaunch.net
Cover concept by Laurie Mandel
Edited by Elizabeth Lyons
Author photo by Monica Philbin

Show Up for Yourself / Janet Philbin. —1st ed.

ISBN 978-1-7344043-2-6 (pbk)
ISBN 978-1-7344043-3-3 (eBook)

"Through the sharing of her own personal experiences and her unique articulation of the therapeutic process, Janet Philbin takes us on a journey of healing and self-discovery. Janet clearly guides us through the darkness of the hurting child within us, through the dark tunnel and into the light of our own self love and self-acceptance. She does all of this by creating a seamless road map that we can all follow to the destination of our highest and truest selves. Dare to meet your most authentic self with Janet's powerful guidance!"

—*Suzi Lula, Spiritual Therapist, Bestselling author of* The Motherhood Evolution: How Thriving Mothers Raise Thriving Children

"Janet Philbin's story of self-healing and awakening is a fascinating one. She demonstrates through her own experiences how to identify our True Self by understanding the wounds of our inner child. *Show Up for Yourself* explains how we express those wounds in our everyday lives and covers ways of transforming them into self-love and acceptance. As you follow her journey, you soon realize that she has shown the reader a beautiful path to self-discovery. Through the process of love, understanding, forgiveness. and release, she incorporates spirituality, energy work, the unconscious, and the Higher Self to create healing at the cellular level. This is a must-read for anyone who is looking for insight and direction in creating meaningful change in their life."

—*William S. Bezmen, Ph.D, PMH, CNS, Founder of HypnoSynergistic & AN RA Energy Healing*

"To heal emotional wounds, especially ones from childhood, is a challenging but incredible journey worth traveling. Janet Philbin shares with her readers not only her own personal experiences but gives wonderful insight and guidance for those who are seeking to heal on many levels. She shines Light on how we deserve happiness and how we can discover the gifts that are within. Her story describes her freeing herself from the wounds of the past in order to live her most genuine and creative life. This book will open your eyes and your heart to the unlimited potential of your inner mind while uncovering the beauty of your soul. Thank you, Janet, for writing this book and sharing your insights and experiences with us."

—*Judith Grant MSN.ANP, Co-Founder of Pathways To Health*

"Janet's book, *Show Up for Yourself*, is a magical journey into the heart. This book is a priceless gift for those who have faced challenges, pain, trauma, and uncertainty in their lives. As Janet says, 'The pain of our past is the pain of our present.' If you want to heal your wounds, ease the burden on your heart, and live your best, most fulfilled and healthy life from this moment forward, you simply MUST get your copy today!"

—*Erin Taylor, MA, Parent Coach, Author, Podcast Host*

"It was truly an honor to read an advance copy of Janet Philbin's new book, *Show Up for Yourself, A Guide To Inner Growth and Awareness*. Janet has an incredible way of drawing her reader into the 'story' with her brilliant writing style. I love how she shares her expertise, wisdom, and knowledge through anecdotes, education, tools, ideas, and her own growth experiences as well as those of her clients. It captivates the reader to want to know and learn more. Throughout her book, Janet offers the reader many opportunities to transform, transcend, and dig deeper into anything that might be hiding underneath. She does this so beautifully and effectively. Offering space for journal entries, pausing, and meditative moments, Janet creates additional opportunities for her readers to process and grow, step by step. Anyone who reads this beautiful work of art will find that there is much healing opportunity within, offered from a place of compassion and kindness that you can feel through each word on the page, encouraging the reader to connect with their truth, their light, and their heart. You will truly feel empowered. Thank you, Janet!

—*Sue DeCaro, Worldwide Coach and Conscious Educator Helping Entrepreneurs, Parents, Individuals, and Corporations*

"If you are curious about energy and healing and know you need to do the inner work but don't know where to begin, look no further. In *Show Up For Yourself*, Janet Philbin has put together an extraordinarily rich tapestry of a book that seamlessly blends all you need to know about energy work, hypnosis, the chakras, and Eastern and Western psychological teachings to help you truly feel, heal, grow, and live your most authentic life. These teachings can be complicated and confusing to comprehend, never mind try to put into any form of practice, but this book is different. It helps demystify it with ease, and with each page turned helps bring about the clarity you have been hungry for. Not only that, it is full of practical and actionable steps and guidance to help the reader reach deep within themselves, do the work, and so begin their healing journey. Once I started, I could not put it down. However, on completing, I know I'll be revisiting and rereading many times. This book is a definitely keeper, for this work is never done and I know it will continue to be a welcome companion to me on my journey.

—*Louise Clarke, Podcast host of Parenting in the Thick of it and author of* Parenting the Modern Teen

"*Show up for yourself* shares essential tools for harnessing the power of our minds and hearts to navigate the ocean into self-growth and transformation. Janet shares a path to healing from both her personal experiences and her clinical work. This is a book that will allow you to flow through its pages, breaking down concepts and practices that are accessible to anyone that wants to embark on a journey to awareness of inner wounds and befriend life's experiences. When life's challenges start to distract you from yourself, please begin here."

—Msc. Andrea González, Clinical Psychologist, Conscious Parent Coach. Former President of the Guatemalan Psychological Association

Contents

To my mom, Jackie. Love you.

ACKNOWLEDGEMENTS

My children continue to be my greatest teachers. As a parent, I continue to learn daily about the struggles of coming into my own as an adult. When I reflect, I am not sure how I made the transition from a high school graduate at seventeen years old to a graduate school graduate at twenty-three years old. It happened, and I know I put in the work to make it happen. I recall being very goal focused and, as my friends tease, practical, but I do not remember the details of the day-to-day ins and outs of what actually occurred in those important years when I had to show up for myself.

My children, who, at the time of this writing, are both approaching and in young adulthood are teaching me this lesson. I watch them having to make "big" decisions in life. I watch them struggle with choices that, to them, seem enormous and are believed to carry so much weight in terms of how their lives will turn out. It is scary, and I think many can identify with this fear—the "what ifs" when making important decisions: "What if I make the wrong choice?" "What if I don't get the job?" "What if I mess up the interview?" And the big one: "What if I change my mind after putting in all this work?"

What I have learned is that, no matter what, we must show up for ourselves. If you do not show up for yourself, no one will. No one can do it for you. I can support my children, be a mirror for them, and be a place for them to test things out, but I cannot show up for them nor can I do the work for them.

After I finished writing the first draft of this book, I struggled with the title. The title feels so important. Anyone looking at the title should be drawn to pick up this book. The first title I wanted to use was *You Have Not Lost Your Mind*. It represented the way I was feeling as I was getting the book out of my head and onto the computer. It was cute, funny, and catchy, but in the end, it was inauthentic to the message of the book. The message really is about showing up for yourself (hence the final title), and I am honored you have picked up the book. My hope is that it offers you a way to show up for yourself in your life that brings you joy, balance, and peace.

This book is to help each of us remember to do just that: show up for ourselves. I offer a framework for how you can show up each and every day. Each day as you open your eyes you have a choice to make. You can choose to show up and greet the day with whatever it brings, or you can choose to be passive and allow the day to be in charge of you. This book is a guide for your inner awareness, growth, and becoming as you step forward in showing up for you.

This book was a labor of love. It was a labor of commitment to myself that began five years prior to it being published. There are many people to acknowledge for their help and support in getting this book out of my head and onto paper.

I owe my love of reading to my mom, to whom this book is dedicated. Mom had a solid command of the English language and was my first editor in life. She never went anywhere without a book, and always had between ten and twenty books waiting to be read at home. She loved mysteries and historical fiction the most. I know if she were here to witness this book's publication, published, she would be beyond proud.

To my husband, Steve. You have always been there for me, supporting all of my explorations, retreats, and adventures of self-discovery and healing. No matter what, I know I am always able to count on you to keep me steady in a storm. Your calm is a definite balance to my high-strung energy. You have sacrificed your own needs at times to support me in my goals. You encouraged me to push forward with this book, always giving me the room and time for the creative process that I needed to allow this book to come through me and onto the pages. Words cannot fully express my deep love for you.

To my children, Monica, Justin, and Amy. You also have been huge supports and cheerleaders for me. You have allowed me to practice on you and run ideas by you, and you always gave me room as your mom to learn how to be a better human. I have to give a shout out to Amy, who is responsible for the graphics in this book. She gets credit for the flowcharts and the chakra picture. I am not great with technology, and Amy was the one who got it done.

To my book coach, editor, and publisher, Elizabeth

Lyons of Finn-Phyllis Press. Thank you. You have been there for me from the start. You had faith in me and in this project. You let me know that what I had to write was valuable, important, and needed. That I had a unique voice to offer the conversation of healing the inner child. Thank you for essentially holding my hand and guiding me through the process of becoming a published author. I know that no one would be reading these pages had it not been for your wisdom, guidance, support, and expertise.

To Dr. Shefali Tsabary, thank you for writing the foreword. Reading your book, *The Awakened Family*, was a catapult that propelled me forward to finally put all the pieces together. Having the opportunity to be a student in your Conscious Parenting Coaching Institute allowed me to deep dive into learning how to deconstruct consciousness. I am honored to call you my teacher, colleague, and friend.

I must also acknowledge my teachers, mentors, and friends, William Bezmen, Ph.D. and Judith Grant, N.P., the owners of Pathways to Health, an integrative and holistic healing center. I completed all of my hypnosis, intuitive and, energy healing training with them and have spent countless hours training and learning under their wise and generous guidance. The chapters on the chakras and hypnosis are laced with the wisdom I have gleaned and put into practice because of the time I spent learning from and with them. What they have taught me has become part of me. After all these years, it is just knowledge that is within me and flows through me.

There are multiple case studies shared within the book. All names and details have been changed to protect confidentiality. I want to thank my many clients over the years. You trusted me with your heart. That is something I do not take lightly. I have learned from you as you have learned from me.

I also must express my deep gratitude to Harriette Ferguson, LCSW. I met Harriette twenty-six years ago, and it was because of her that I was able to get my private practice started. She always had faith and trust in me. Harriette referred to me my first client, and I bartered with her for her office space early on Saturday mornings. Harriette has been my supervisor, mentor, and friend. She is a brilliant clinician and the author of *What to Expect When You're Experiencing Infertility: How to Cope with the Emotional Crisis and Survive*. Her help, guidance, support, and skills have been a constant over the span of my career as a clinician. I am proud to call her my friend and colleague.

To my sisters, Karen and Lorie. There has been no greater relationship than the one we share as sisters. You are irreplaceable. Our shared experiences of growing up are forever etched in my heart and mind. Our childhood was the blueprint for who I am today. Thank you for always being there for me, supporting me, and having my back. Love you both so much.

To my close friends, and you know who you are, thank you for standing by my side, never judging me. You have always accepted me, even when you may not have fully understood my reasons for moving forward in one direction versus another. My heart is full knowing you are by my side.

The cover design was inspired by my favorite artist and dear friend, Laurie Mandel, Ed.D. Laurie is a gifted artist and she brought my vision of a book cover into something that captured the energy and intention of the material contained in these pages. You can see more of her art at sageartstudios.com.

Welcome to the sacred journey into yourself. Thank you for allowing me to be by your side.

You are a co-creator of your reality. You always have been—you just haven't fully been aware of it. By repeating patterns of the past, you have been unconsciously reacting to the present moment. These unconscious reactions set the present moment in a particular way, and in so doing, they also set your future in a particular way. These unconscious reactions are the part you play in the co-creation of your reality. This powerful book paves an understanding of how to shift from an unconscious co-creator to a conscious one.

Each of us bears the emotional legacies of our childhood. Many of these keep us chained to the past, encumbered by debilitating belief systems that keep us mired in fear. As we begin to heal ourselves, the inner self grows into wholeness and greater consciousness, allowing us to make choices of empowerment and clarity. In this way, we release from the past and begin to walk to a new tomorrow.

Healing is a journey, and it is work. Many do not want to do the work. Many do not want to look at their old, painful memories. Deconstructing your patterns and healing your inner child requires commitment. There is no magic wand that any therapist or coach can wave to "fix" what you feel needs to be repaired. Memories from childhood helped to shape who we are today and how we cope with the stressors in our lives. As adults, we continuously (and subconsciously) act out the recurring patterns formed through our families of origin and ancestral patterns because we simply do not know another way. Until we awaken and begin to evolve, we cannot begin to break these patterns. It is up to each and every one of us to do this work for ourselves.

We all need help to heal - whether through wisdom-teachers, self-help courses, or meditation journeys. This book offers a bit of all three: wisdom, a self-directed path toward change and action, and ways to go inward in a meditative way. It is a call to action and accountability in raising your inner self into wholeness and health. It will greatly support you on your path toward living as your most authentic self.

In this wonderful book, Janet will take you on a deep journey within yourself. Through the use of storytelling, personal experiences, meditation practices, and journal exercises, she will help you ignite your greatest vision for yourself. In these pages you will find inspiration to break patterns you have been stuck in and discover a wealth of courage to make huge transformations in your life.

Your journey towards your truest self begins here. Your power is waiting to be claimed. You are deserving of its many gifts.

Shefali Tsabary, Ph.D.
Clinical Psychologist, bestselling author

INTRODUCTION

When I was twenty-two and a graduate social work student at New York University, I took a class in child developmental psychology. As the class continued, I became more and more aware that parts of me were becoming increasingly uncomfortable. I began having feelings, thoughts, and memories that were interfering with both my studies and my life in general. This was the first time I'd ever had this kind of disruptive emotional experience, and it took a few months of not understanding before I realized what was happening: My own childhood trauma was getting poked and woken up, and those memories and feelings were interfering with my life.

The specific details are not important because we each have our own traumas, and the point is that we learn to heal from our pain and trauma. We are not here to judge one person's trauma as worse than or less than another's. Your trauma is your experience, and healing is possible, no matter the source of it.

At the time, not knowing exactly how to handle this disruption, I did what every aware, budding social worker would do: I opened the Yellow Pages (the Google of yesteryear, for those who never used them), found a social worker, and made an appointment. The work to heal my inner child began. While I did not know it at the time, it was the beginning of a long and incredible journey. A journey that has had more layers than I can count. A journey that has brought me more tears than I thought I could ever shed. A journey that has paired me with some very skilled healers and professionals. A journey that opened me up to gifts I didn't even know I possessed. A journey that led me onto my true spiritual path.

None of these end results was expected. All of them were things I would rather have avoided had I been given a choice when it came to whether or not to live through my trauma in the first place. But I did live through it, and now, thirty years later, I can look back and declare that I am in gratitude for that trauma. Without it, I would not be where I am now. I would not be writing these words. I would not be brave enough to be vulnerable. I have recently crossed some kind of threshold into a new part of myself, and while this part is still developing, I know it is growing; I know it is becoming. It is a part that is real, raw, and can touch the truth of the deepest parts of my soul.

I have come to believe that I came into this life as Janet for a purpose—to heal myself, to heal my soul, and to be a catalyst of healing for others. To use my own journey through healing to light the way for others. To those who are afraid of their deep pain, to those who are afraid of their feelings, to those who are afraid of talking to the inner child who lives inside of them, I am here to tell you that you are not alone. I know it might feel like you've been alone for a very long time, suffering in silence, but you are no longer alone. I write these pages about healing for your inner child, just as I write them for mine. You see, when you give that inner child a voice that can be heard outside of your head, *you* become the one with the power instead of the voice. You can hear out loud the faulty thoughts, the lies, the stories, the fears, and the love. You are allowed to speak it. Speaking it gives you freedom. It is time to be free. Haven't you been held as a prisoner of the past for long enough? Haven't the stories of the past ruled your life and made your decisions for long enough? If so, you are reading the right book.

In this book, you are going to learn to dig in. You are going to come to understand that healing is a spiral that expands upward. It also goes around and around, and as a result, we have to keep touching some of the same points over and over again. But, each time we're doing so from a higher—or move evolved—point. Each time we go up a level on the Spiral of Healing, when we touch that old, soft, and painful spot again, it does not hurt as much as it did before. We look at it from a different perspective and realize with each new look that we are healing. That we are growing. That our true self is emerging.

We will look at it for the inner child inside each of us, and we will help him or her. That little one will no longer have to be alone, scared, hiding, shameful, or fearful. Nor will they have to feel unworthy, unlovable, unimportant, or not enough. Yes, it will take time. Yes, you will need to dedicate yourself to you. But I am here to tell you that it is possible. You *can* heal. You *can* feel better. You no longer have to let the pain of the past dictate your present or inform your future.

This is a magical journey into the self, into the heart, to look at the parts that are in need of love, compassion, and healing. To learn to give yourself that which seems easier to give to another. Imagine feeling less anxious. Imagine yelling less at your spouse, partner, or children. Imagine feeling calm and balanced. It is possible.

There is a disclaimer: It will not be easy. The road will be full of ups and downs. It will be one on which, at times, you will need to take a break and regroup before starting again. I will guide you through it. The reason all of this is so important is that *you* are important. You matter. You are worth it.

My road to this point has not been straight—not by a long shot. I did not know I was embarking upon a curvy, bumpy, confusing road when I started. I figured I'd just go to a therapist, talk about it, and feel better. Even as a social work student, I didn't *really* get it. I didn't get that, in order to heal, you must *go through.* You must go through the pain in order to emerge into the light on the other side and find your *own* light—the one that resides inside you. The light is always there waiting for you as you plough through the darkness of your pain.

My crazy, crooked, bumpy journey began with that slight feeling of discomfort. When I recognized that my past--the one that I thought I had wrapped up neatly in a box and hidden behind a big brick wall—was interfering in my day-to-day life, I knew I needed help. There is no shame in needing help, though if I am being honest, I did feel shame at the time. I was not honest with my roommate as to why I was suddenly leaving an hour earlier for my field placement. It took me a few months to tell her I was in counseling, and when I did tell her, thankfully she was supportive. Because my own personal trauma was filled with shame, so was every action I took that was connected with it. I was petrified that if I shared that I was in counseling, I would also have to share the reason why. My therapist helped me understand that I did not have to share the why, and once I told my roommate, my stress levels went down because it was one less secret I had to keep. Each step of the way was a learning process for me—a learning process about myself. And that is what this book will be for you—a learning process about *yourself*.

One of the ways we will be digging in is through learning to understand how we carry our emotions in our physical body. We will explore the chakra system to understand why we hold certain emotions in specific parts of our human bodies. We will also learn ways to help remove the pain from our human bodies.

We will blend Eastern philosophy and Western psychology along the way, as I believe that there is an important place for both in healing. We will redefine what a trigger is and begin to understand it from a new viewpoint. We will explore what healing is and how it is a spiral that we travel, one which I believe we travel upwards. We will go through the Spiral of Healing framework, which includes the components of feel, heal, love, and grow. We will talk about the inner child, the false self, and the ego. We will talk about how the inner child develops and why he or she is still impacting your day-to-day life as an adult. We will be journaling as well as talking about and practicing meditation (not to mention gaining a clear understanding as to why both are so important), and finally, learning the steps you can take to heal the pain of your inner child so you can blossom into the amazing light you came here to be.

You will find journal prompts in many of the chapters with space to do your journaling directly in this book. The prompts are purposeful, intended to help you explore your own inner world more deeply. This book is here to be a companion on your journey to heal. If you are reading the eBook version, dedicate a journal for this purpose. Take notes as you go. Write in the book. Allow this book to become living evidence of your healing journey.

Getting the thoughts out of your head and onto paper is a big piece of the transformative process. While I won't say that journaling is mandatory to your success, I would like to. Journaling lets you see your "stuff"; it releases it from your cells and gives you a chance to process all the thoughts and stories you usually keep in your head. Because, guess what? Keeping it in your head causes stress and anxiety. If you want to feel less anxious and less stress, journal.

"We heal from the inside out" has been the philosophy by which I've practiced as a clinician over the past thirty years. So, please know that I am not offering you a how-to with a step-by-step guide that you must follow and without which you cannot heal. Instead, I am offering you the learned wisdom of my professional and personal journeys. I am offering you *a* way. There are many ways out there; just go look at the self-help section of any bookstore. That is why this is not so much a how-to book as it is a why-now book.

Why now are you ready to heal? Why now are you ready to dive in and gain a deeper understanding of yourself? Why now are you ready to roll up your sleeves and dig in to do this work of honoring your true self in order to become the one you arrived here on this Earth to be? It is not up to me to answer your questions or solve your problems. It is up to me to give you the tools to enable you to be your own seamstress, to heal the parts that need mending. Remember, you are not broken, there is nothing to fix. There are only parts of you that need love and attention. I am honored that you have chosen to journey with me into your healing.

Throughout this book, I will share insights that I have gained while in meditation. Once you choose to open to your intuitive gifts, you will begin to "hear" insights that are meant specifically for you. The collective consciousness, source energy, and universal wisdom is there for all of us to tap into. These insights were meant for me, and they were also meant for you.

To get started on this journey, I want to share an insight, an inner knowing, I had during a recent meditation:

It is up to us to know the wisdom within us, for this is something no one else can teach us. We must be our own

guiding light. There is no competition with another. Any
thoughts of competition come from the false self, and this
belief lives in the place that holds the belief that you are
not enough. If you are the belief that you are not enough,
then you look at others and believe they are more than
you, doing it better than you, more gifted and more talent-
ed. This leads to competition with them, but that competi-
tion is one in which you are against yourself.

You see, there is nothing and no one better than you, and
that is because there is only one you—one you with the
very unique and special gifts that you came here to share.
Be in abundance. There is more than enough for everyone.
Everyone has the potential to tap into the abundance.
When you do not feel worthy, you will fill your internal
holes with external fillers, and doing so dulls your light.
Some do this through the use of alcohol, drugs, food, TV,
or social media, and in doing so, they become numb to
their own truth.

There is a false belief that touching your truth will be
painful, and you hold this belief because you do not know
the true self within.

The true self lives inside your heart.
This one is the truth of the who that you are.

This one is protected from pain by limiting beliefs, and
therefore, cannot easily be touched. All of your gifts wait
for you to be ready to awaken, evolve, and become. Ready

to begin to live, value, and cherish yourself.

The true self inside of you is a beacon of light, much like a rudder designed to hold you steady in a storm. But, you must step up and become the captain of your ship. It is up to the you in the now to get back into the driver's seat of your life. To not be afraid of the pain--the pain of going through healing is not worse than the trauma you have already survived. Be the light that you are. Come on a journey of exploration and self-care, and let's find the hidden treasures that are you, that reside within you. Let's awaken to your true potential and calling.

IN THE BEGINNING

How the heck did all this start, anyway? I mean, how did a girl like me, educated in a traditional social work school, wind up in a space such as this? It actually all began when I was seventeen and first stepped foot onto what would become my college campus for the next four years. That college was Springfield College in Massachusetts.

As I got onto campus, I saw the triangle with the motto, "Spirit, Mind, and Body". Little did I know, that motto would actually become the framework for my healing practice. I didn't know that those three words—spirit, mind, and body--actually meant something when they were connected. That, when connected, they have a powerful healing ability. They can be transformative within and for us. They enable us to get in touch with the true essence of who we are. You can connect with your inner light to help yourself, and in that connection, you are able to heal yourself. Once we do that, we have overflow that allows us to help others. Springfield is a service-oriented college. They want their students to get out into the community to be helpers, change makers, and leaders, and when we do our own internal work on spirit, mind, and body, that can actually happen. Let me break this motto down as I understand it.

The mind is in school to learn. Okay, so thankfully I was in the right place. But one thing I did *not* know when I arrived at Springfield was the importance of the body when it comes to healing (or anything else!). It seemed that everyone I met at freshman orientation was an athlete in some way—on a sports team or a fan of exercising on their own. The first question I was asked after introducing myself at orientation was, "What sport do you play?" I remember being taken aback, wondering why I was being asked this. I didn't play any sports. I was a drama kid in high school. It wasn't since fifth grade when, on a dare from a boy in my class, I joined the town baseball league, which had just opened to girls. I was one of two girls who played that year, just to prove I could do it.

When asked about sports at Springfield, I began telling people I was an "un-jock," someone who didn't exercise or play sports. People looked at me with disbelief. How could this be, and why would I choose this school if that were the case? Well, the answer to that question was, the school chose me. As I pulled onto campus my senior year of high school for a tour and caught my first sighting of

Naismith Hall (I later learned that basketball was invented there), I saw the ivy growing up the brick building and something inside me exploded. It was a feeling of knowing "This is it." That was the spirit part. This was my college; this was where I belonged. Unbeknownst to me, I had stepped into my first experience of spirit as part of the mind, body, spirit connection. The college was my training ground, my becoming, my learning to listen to my inner voice.

The next time I listened to my inner voice was during my sophomore year. I entered Springfield with an unde-clared major, hoping to get into the physical therapy pro-gram. But, by the end of freshman year, I accepted that, although I liked science, I did not have a science brain. I declared gerontology, which was a sociology program, as my major. As such, I found myself in a class called Intro to Social Welfare. Usually, intro classes are boring, right? Well, this class was taught by a Columbia-University-trained social worker named Dr. Miriam Hirsch. I sat down in her class and was immediately hooked. I read that text-book like it was the best fiction novel ever, drinking up every word. To this day, I recall sitting at the desk in my dorm room, which sat in front of the window, knowing that I had found what I loved. Once again, that same feel-ing came over me, that same inner knowing, this time re-lated to my career choice. I would be a social worker. I took every class Dr. Hirsch taught, and she became my mentor and a great friend. Thirty years later, my Intro to Social Welfare textbook still sits on my shelf as a reminder to trust my inner knowing. At the time, I didn't know what I was trusting; I just knew it felt good, so I followed it and trusted myself enough to do so.

When I entered social work school in late 1989, very few people were talking about utilizing hypnosis and spirituality in clinical work with clients. In fact, within the entirety of my two years in the MSW program at New York University, I did not hear the word hypnosis or spirituality uttered once in connection to social work practice. Therefore, neither was on my radar as a young social worker, fresh out of graduate school.

My career began in a city hospital in Queens, NY. My very first patient on the medical/surgical floor to which I was assigned was detoxing from alcohol. She was hallucinating while I conducted her psychosocial assessment. You can only imagine how well that went, as she described to me that my teeth were as long as my body, reaching my knees, and asked me about my hair, wondering where it all went. I was twenty-two years old, and I had never seen anyone detox before. I went back to the head nurse, totally confused and needing to ask what was going on.

Working at a city hospital in 1991 was a wonderful learning ground for me. It allowed me to be a part of the beginning of cutting-edge treatment for people living with AIDS. AZT was new, and we had a lot of hope for its use by those in the AIDS community. As a medical social worker, many of my patients were diagnosed with AIDS, and we were still at the relative beginning of the AIDS epidemic. I wound up working with many patients who were doing their best to live with the disease. I loved working with this population and was lucky enough to transfer and become one of the social workers on the AIDS team at the hospital. This time period marked the beginning of my true understanding of life and death.

What I learned was that I loved the work. I remember my patients with so much fondness and compassion, for they were my first true teachers. Many wound up with AIDS as a result of their own behaviors. I had to learn to sit in compassion, not judge, deeply see another's pain, and understand that, even as someone is dying, they can still live. My patients also taught me that, even though they were living with AIDS, that fact did not mean they would die from AIDS.

One of my responsibilities was to lead a support group for my patients. They would come each week and speak about their struggles, fears, families, life, and death. One week, one of the women in the group didn't come. I already knew she would not be there. I had to tell the group that their friend had died that week. Not from AIDS, but from an asthma attack. This brought the message home for me as well as for them. Yes, AIDS was, at that time, a death sentence. The AIDS cocktails were new, and the future was uncertain. But what each of us learned that week was that *all* of our futures are uncertain, whether or not we were living with AIDS. The lesson was "Live now, heal now." Or, as they would say, "Deal with your shit."

We learned that a diagnosis did not necessarily mean one's death would occur in the way they anticipated it,

and if we could not be certain of that, we must take responsibility for how we live. I began to learn that we must
heal in the now. I was already learning that, in my personal
life, I needed to work out my "shit," but I was coming to
understand that my bigger mission was to help others heal
theirs.

Fast forward a few years, I left the city hospital and
went to work in long-term geriatric care. It was my dream
job. I had an amazing relationship with my grandparents
and wanted to be able to work with the elderly. Once
again, I found myself working in the trenches of death and
dying. In fact, I became the facility's hospice social worker
when the program was started. I loved the work. I loved
my old people. I loved being with them, helping the families, and bearing witness with them as their lives came to
an end.

It was different than my AIDS work, as my residents
lived into their seventies, eighties, and nineties. They lived
full lives and their deaths made sense, as much as any
death can, because they reflected the natural order of life.
Their deaths were no less painful for their families, but I
was able to help, to be there at a crucial time when my
patients and families needed the most emotional support.

I again learned a great deal about both life and death
working with my residents. They had so much wisdom to
share and advice to give. Giving them your ear and opening your heart to them allowed them emotional comfort
and healing in their final stages of life. I learned the importance of speaking your truth, saying what needs to be

said, and giving someone permission to leave this Earth. People would often ask me how I could do that work with the dying, and my answer was always, "How could I not?" I have found that the most sacred place to be is at someone's bedside as they take their last breath. It is hard, and it is sacred. What other life event, other than birth, has such significance? Being with someone in that moment is to be present, to be fully present, and it's what caused me to learn first-hand about the importance of being fully present in each moment, especially the hard ones.

It was 1999, and my husband and I had just had our second baby in seventeen months. Yup, we went from no kids to two in a very short period of time. Through a series of events, I wound up getting the opportunity to begin my own private psychotherapy practice. I bartered for office space and began seeing my first client once a week for $25. I had just that one client for the first eight months before I got a second, and then a third. I let my practice grow organically into whatever it was supposed to become. I had two babies at home, and I didn't want to work more hours than I could handle.

My practice grew, and within two or three years, I was seeing between nine and twelve clients a week. Things were good. I was specializing in infertility, which, like death, is steeped in grief and loss, and so I knew that I was right where I needed to be.

In 2002, I was coming into the awareness that I was

feeling "stuck" with some clients. I just could not help them break through certain emotional sticking points to a deeper place of self-understanding. I specifically recall one client sitting across from me on the couch, telling me of her deep feelings of aloneness. No matter how we tried to explore it, we could not get under this feeling or help her get any relief from it. While I stuck with her, as a trained therapist, I was feeling quite ineffective and didn't know what other approaches to try.

A short time after, a piece of mail arrived that would alter the course of my career. The one thing about the office I was occupying was that the mail service was unreliable; mail often got lost or never arrived at all. Because of this, I had all my work mail sent to my home address. One day, I received a letter about a 100-hour hypnotherapy certification course being offered at a center not too far away from me called Pathways to Health. The owners of the center, William Bezmen, Ph.D. and Judith Grant, NP, would eventually become my mentors and friends. I was trained by William in the transformational hypnotherapy process that I now practice.

Hypnosis intrigued me, and I began to wonder if it was an effective way to help me help my clients more effectively so they could truly heal their inner wounds. My only experience with hypnosis up to that point occurred in college. I was one of those twenty-year-old college students who, when the stage hypnotist performing at the bar my friends and I were at asked for volunteers from the audience, I raised my hand and got picked to go up on stage.

Now, if you have ever seen a stage hypnotist, you may have noticed that they ask questions, testing a potential participant to see how susceptible she is to being hypnotized. They of course do not want anyone on stage who will resist. Well, I passed the test. I do not recall all of the experience, but I will share what I do recall because it made a lasting impression.

The first thing that happened once I was on stage was that I asked if I could run and use the bathroom; I was drinking, after all. The hypnotist said no, touched the center of my forehead with his finger, and said I would no longer need to use the bathroom. He said I'd be comfortably able to wait until the end of the show. I did, in fact, become comfortable. He proceeded with the show and had all of us doing the silly things stage hypnotists do to entertain the crowd. I was told that I had a little bird on my index finger, and I was holding out my finger so the bird could sit on it like a perch. Then, he said the bird was starting to shit, and I had to shake it off my hand. I remember shaking my hand so hard trying to get that damn bird shitting on me *off* of me! It did not come off, and I did not stop shaking my finger until he said to stop. The last thing I recall is, we were told that after we left the stage and got back to our seats, he would give a command to wake us up. As we heard the command word spoken, we were to kiss the guy or girl closest to us, and we would then be dehypnotized. I left the stage, went back to my seat at the bar with my friends, and a few minutes later, the hypnotist called out the word. I remember reaching over to the guy next to me, whom I did not know, and planting a kiss on his lips. The bar was hysterical with laughter, as was I because I was in disbelief that I just kissed this random guy. Then, seemingly out of the blue, I had to make a run for the lady's room because I thought my bladder was going to explode. Needless to say, all the ladies let me cut the line.

Getting back to the letter that arrived in the mail, I knew hypnosis had at one time had a profound effect on me, so I called and spoke to the William, who taught the class. After our brief conversation, I signed up for the 100-hour training, and four months later became a certified hypnotherapist.

I should also mention that when I arrived at the center for the first day of the course, they asked how I heard of them. I said, "You mailed me a flyer." They looked for my name on the mailing list and had no record of me. Before that letter arrived by mail, I'd never heard of them. Remember, it was 2002, and the internet was not as robust as it is today. In fact, most businesses at the time were new to having a website, if they had one at all. It was the era of snail mail and phone calls. I was floored, as were they, that I wound up there to take the class. This was a lesson for me in the Divine synchronicity of the universe. I already held the belief that things happen for a reason because of all of my experiences working with the dying, but I had not had such a personally synchronistic experience before. I did not know it at the time, but this "chance" encounter with a piece of mail showing up to an address that was known to clients only as "the place where Janet's office is" would mark a turning point in my professional and personal lives.

The reason it marked such a turning point had a great deal to do with the fact that Pathways to Health is a complementary health center with a focus on spirituality. As a clinician, I simply wanted to learn the clinical aspects of hypnosis so that I would be able to do the work with my clients to help them heal. When my instructor, William, started speaking about energy, angels, guides, becoming an An-Ra energy healer and the like, I tuned out. That part wasn't for me. I didn't really believe in any of it, and I wanted no part in any of the other classes they taught at the center (which had a strong spiritual focus). However, through this training, I was exposed to the center and its beliefs even though I was strongly resistant. I was closed off to anything outside of the traditional therapy box beyond what I was there to learn through hypnosis training.

As I began to practice hypnotherapy with my clients, I began to see big changes. All of a sudden, instead of my client being stuck in her feeling of being alone, we were able to go back into her childhood and find out when and why that feeling began and heal her younger self, or, as we refer to it, her inner child. Fascinated that the hypnosis was working, I also began using it with my infertility patients, and watched with delight as they began coping better with the stress of fertility treatments—as well as that of finally getting pregnant. Obviously, I cannot say, "Do hypnosis and you will get pregnant" any more than a doctor can say, "Do IVF and you will get pregnant." What I can say, however, is that hypnosis helped my patients improve in their ability to cope with the stress and loss during their fertility journeys. They improved their coping skills, learned about the mind/body connection, and were less stressed during their treatment cycles. I like to believe that all of these changes combined increased their odds of becoming pregnant.

I was also doing hypnosis with patients who had other medical diagnoses. An experience with one client with whom I worked three years after getting my certification forever changed the course of my practice and belief systems. This woman, whom I will refer to as Ruth, had ulcerative colitis and had been gravely ill with C-difficile in the months before she came to see me. Ruth wanted to use hypnosis and guided imagery to help her heal the colitis. As irony would have it, I had a chaise lounge in my office, so my clients would lie on this chaise lounge during hypnosis, and I would wheel over in my desk chair and sit next to them. During one session, I sat next to Ruth with my palms facing up. We had been working together for a while and were making progress, and during our session, I felt a sensation I can only describe as energy come down to my palms. It was palpable. It had a texture and a temperature. And, because I knew about energy from Pathways, I believed that's what it was. I did nothing about it and simply continued with her session. This experience continued to happen when I had sessions with her, and when I could no longer fight it, I gave in and accepted that this energy was coming to me in order that I would feel it, be aware of it, and honor it. It was time for me to honor it as a gift that was opening itself up for me. This marked the beginning of my spiritual awakening and my journey combining that awakening with my hypnotherapy practice. The way I was able to combine energy healing into my hypnotherapy practice was by becoming a master An-Ra energy healer. This powerful method of energy healing, developed by William Bezmen and Judith Grant, works with the chakras to balance, clear, and heal the client's energetic bodies.

This book is a result of the unexpected and miraculous learnings that I've come to know throughout my time working with clients as well as doing the work necessary to heal my own inner child. Now that you have some background on my quest to deeply understand and heal the inner child, let's dive in more deeply to *your* healing, starting with your relationship with yourself.

PART 1

WHO IS SHOWING UP?

CHAPTER 1

Conscious Relationship with Self

By this point in my life, I've been doing inner work for more of my life than not. In 2016, I found Dr. Shefali Tsabary's book, *The Awakened Family*. The first sentence of the first paragraph of the book reads, "We awaken when we become aware of who we truly are (p.1)." That was all I needed to read. My heart skipped a beat, and I knew in that moment that I had found a home where I could put together all I had learned in one place in order to finally complete the healing work I was already doing with my clients. As importantly, I knew that this would affect my own healing as well.

Dr. Shefali's approach is called Conscious Parenting. I recall going to her conference, Evolve, for the first time in 2017. While at dinner with a new friend, we discussed the concept of Conscious Parenting. After sharing the trans-formational hypnotherapy I conduct with clients, I stated that I knew that Conscious Parenting and hypnotherapy went together like puzzle pieces. My challenge, at the time, was that I didn't know how to make them properly fit together. I was, for sure, intent on figuring it out.

Fast-forward to February 2019 when I was accepted into the first cohort of Dr. Shefali's Conscious Parenting Coaching Method Institute. I knew in my bones that this was the deep dive I needed to be able to fit the puzzle pieces together once and for all. Since graduating from the program, that is exactly what I have done. You do not need to be a parent to do this work because it is not our children who cause us the pain we need to heal from; it is our own inner child who is in pain and needs healing. Therefore, if you have ever had a parent, and all of us have, you qualify. Almost all of us were raised by unconscious parents—people who were parenting from their own places of internal pain. People who parented like their parents before them. These are generational patterns that need to be broken. Until we awaken, we will continue to parent and be in relationships with our old coping mechanisms in place because we haven't yet learned another way. As I will explain throughout the book, the inner child develops as a way to survive in childhood. The hurt part of your inner child wants to heal.

My passion is helping people heal the emotional wounds they carry with them from childhood, because I believe that these wounds get acted out in adulthood. There is a younger self who resides within each of us, and he or she is in pain. I believe that your inner child is looking to heal, and in order to get attention, he or she acts out and becomes depressed, anxious, or disempowered with feelings of low self-confidence or low self-esteem. My goal in writing this book is to help people reconnect with themselves. To know their emotions, to confidently feel their feelings, and to heal. I want to help individuals connect with themselves so they can connect with the people in their lives with whom they are closest, and I firmly believe that the way to do this is through healing one's inner child. To understand the puzzle we will be assembling, you'll need a brief lesson on conscious connecting in relationships as well as with yourself.

Conscious connecting, when it comes to relationships, is for all of us, not only parents. In Conscious Parenting, Dr. Shefali talks about healing the adult, the parent, because in order to consciously connect with another, you must be able to connect with yourself. We have to hold the assumption that, as we heal, as we get to know ourselves better and go through the layers of healing, we will no longer have to "act" out our unmet childhood needs toward those in our lives now.

One of the principles of Conscious Parenting is that a source of the parental pain (or, if you are not a parent, your own pain) stems from the fact that they are fighting the reality that is in front of them instead of accepting that this is the reality *right now*. Do you ever do this in your life? Do you ever fight the reality of what is happening, wishing for it to be different than it is in the moment? We do this in response to fear—a fear that is based on expectations. This fear affects your ability to be able to accept the as-is of the moment.

A critical step in healing occurs when we can accept the as-is of any moment.

I have begun to think, over the years, about the ways the concepts of Conscious Parenting can be applied to other relationships—with self, spouse, partner, parents, friends, co-workers, siblings, and anyone else. I've concluded that the potential for healing relationships is limitless if you are open to the potential of healing yourself (which is also limitless). The end result is, you become more consciously aware of the self. As you do, you take that conscious awareness into every relationship in your life. You can look at each relationship and both see and understand how you are triggered by a variety of outside influences.

Being in a conscious relationship with another is all about connection, and the one you need to be connected to first and foremost is you. You must be in tune with and aware of yourself. You must be aware of what is rising up within you in any given moment and taking care of yourself first by being present and tuned in to your feelings. Pausing and tuning in to your feelings allows you time to understand why you may be reacting in a certain way.

This is why I will later teach you about the chakras. Once you understand the chakra system and the purposeful pause exercise, which we'll discuss in chapter 9, you can begin to take a moment to tune into your body in order to gain an inner awareness of where the feeling making you uncomfortable resides. This is not a quick fix to any problem, but a process of coming back to your true self. It is about understanding the unconscious motivations for your reactivity. When you can become more conscious and bring that quality into your relationships, you can allow for your full range of feelings and emotions. Also, you can allow those in your lives to experience *their* full range of feelings and emotions. You can drop your agenda for the other and truly focus only on the self. Ultimately, the only one you can control is you. When you release the need to control, you can connect. Connection is the key ingredient in Conscious Parenting as well as in having conscious relationships with other people of importance in your life. Most of all, it's critical to having a conscious relationship with yourself.

Being in a conscious relationship with one's self provides the roadmap to growth. Here is one example. "Nagging" is what my almost twenty-year-old son told me I was doing a lot of one day last summer. He was right. As I sat with it, I was able to see my controlling self at the helm, driving the ship that nags. My behaviors weren't new, but I was so appreciative, and it was so beautiful that my son was able to trust our relationship enough to be this honest. He felt emotionally safe to share with me. I owned my behavior and words and told him that I knew it was an issue and something I would continue to work on. I gave him permission to continue to hold me accountable.

Just as a map informs that You Are Here, consciousness says, "Be here. Understand what is going on within you at this moment so it does not impact the next moment in the same way." This was a moment of connection between my son and me. Knowing that filled my heart. In connecting like this, he felt seen and validated. This is the transformative power of being connected in relationships that allow for growth and healing.

As Brené Brown teaches, we are hardwired for love and connection. Without it, we fall apart and have a very hard time knowing how to get back up because we have never developed the internal resources necessary to effectively do so. In this moment of connection and honesty, neither of us had to fall apart; we instead came together.

In essence, the conscious relationship is really the relationship you are able to develop with yourself once you are more aware of your triggers. When you are able to develop this relationship with yourself through inner child healing and hypnosis with the framework of the Spiral of Healing in mind (don't worry, we'll get to that concept in great detail), it will have a positive impact on all of your relationships because you will no longer be acting out from the place of your wounded inner child. You will instead respond from a place of being present and aware in each moment, pausing before you respond to tune in to your own inner world.

CHAPTER 2

My Own Awakening to Spirituality

In 2006 when I was a student taking a course I now teach called "Spiritual Journey Within," we had to do an exercise wherein we closed our eyes and listened to a story that was channeled by Barbara Brennan. As I meditated and listened to this story, I began to see and understand my connection to my light and life in a new way. Here is what happened during that meditation for me:

I saw myself high up in the stars. I remember that the image I saw was Harold, the little boy from the children's book, *Harold and the Purple Crayon,* by Crockett Johnson. Just like Harold, I was able to draw in the stars. I saw myself zipping around in the night sky, zooming from star to star with my crayon, which connected me to the stars and to the universe. I remembered in that moment that I was not alone. That I too was once a star, a light force of energy that was formless. That I came from somewhere greater and brighter, and that I was more connected, whole, and complete than I ever knew before.

People often ask me, "What do you do?" I'd like to answer as though they asked who I *am*, not what I do. I am one who came here to experience life, to heal, to grow, to help. I am one who loves to learn, loves to help others (sometimes too much, because helping can turn into fixing, but I am aware of that and that part of me is a work in progress). I am one who came here to have a human experience with all of the pain and the joy and everything in between. I am one who has come to understand that being and becoming are two different things. Being is an in-the-moment experience; it is presence; it is conscious awareness to the now, to this moment, this second, this breath. The present teaches us that there is no greater moment in time than this moment, the one happening right now. That is being. Becoming, on the other hand, is about the future. It is in the dreams, in the healing, in the growth, in the living, and in the moving. I am one who is human and being and becoming.

So, how do we become one who is being? How do we manifest that? In order to manifest, we must step into the arena and dare greatly, as Brene Brown teaches. We must embrace our vulnerabilities and allow our soft, tender spots to show us the way. Our pain, failings, and upsets do light the way for a deeper understanding of who we are if we let them. Can the darkest parts of ourselves turn on our lights? Can those dark parts also serve as our paths out of pain and show us where we need to go in order to heal?

Are you brave enough to look, to own, to see, and to hear your darkness? I hope so, because in the dark you will find your light. You will see that the light was always there. You came into this human beingness with it, but then life happened. And, if that life was or is filled with pain in the present or was painful in some way in the past, there are some who won't be able to hold onto the light within. The pain is simply too heavy, hard, and dense; the light starts to dim; and then looks as if it has gone out. We forget that we were once light and one with source energy, and we become heavy with the density of life's pain. We may live like that for many years; some may live like that for their entire life. If you are reading this, it means that you re-member—that a part of you remembers that you are light—and you are searching for your way back to your light, to brighten it by reconnecting with source energy.

If this seems a bit "out there," I get it, because I was once in that exact place, and still am sometimes. We are all having an experience as humans doing our best to be. It was because of my pain, my deepest pain, the darkest of places, that I was able to remember the who that I am, which brought me back to my knowing that I was once connected to source light. That I came from something bigger, more magnificent, and brighter than anything I had ever experienced.

Up until the aforementioned meditation wherein I saw myself as Harold, high up in the stars, I had been heavily resistant to any sort of spiritual awakening. I am not even sure I knew there was such a thing as a spiritual awakening. I had done traditional healing work before with an excellent therapist, but I knew that what I was being called to was deeper. I was being called onto my journey to learn, heal, understand, and become.

Looking back, I believe the reason I was resistant to awakening this connection to my light, to source energy, was fear. I knew deep in my cells, deep in my soul, that in order to awaken, I would have to face my deepest fears, look at my deepest shame, and embrace my deepest pain. In order to heal, we are called forth to do the work, and trust me, this was not work I wanted to do. Each time I considered it, the anxiety it stirred up was overwhelming, so I did everything I could to avoid it. But, at that time, I also knew that I could not move forward on my path without going there. It was as if I had reached a stop sign, and instead of saying "Stop," the sign said "Choose a path"—a path forward, through the pain, to reach my light and potential. Otherwise, I had to stay where I was. And for me, at that time, staying where I was wasn't any longer an option. I'd stayed "there" long enough; I was done.

My favorite quote by Anais Nin rose up within me: *"And the day came when the risk to remain tight in a bud was more painful than the risk it took to blossom."* This quote has become a mantra for me, and it pops up whenever it is time for me to go deeper, connect more, and heal. This was the day—the day to start to blossom.

I slowly took in that deep breath, like we do before we dive into deep water, and went down the path. I have no regrets. Facing the darkest parts of my pain has brought me here, and I would not have it any other way. I am still human in my beingness, but I am willing to get up, shake off the dust, and do it all over, again and again, if it means I get to be my light.

A funny thing happens once you begin to awaken to who you really are. You slowly but steadily begin to look at the world with new eyes. You may at times even feel separate and different from those around you. It may feel like they don't get it (or you). But you begin to trust what you are feeling and also feel excited to learn more. That is what happened to me in a most curious way.

Healing is a journey, and an ongoing one at that. I really do not believe that one is never finished healing, growing, and becoming. I, for one, never want to be. If healing creates clarity, brings joy, creates self-compassion, brings inner peace, allows me to experience calm, and keeps me learning, I never want to stop.

Do I believe that awakening to spirituality is a must in order to heal? No, I do not. But what I do believe is that once we open to heal, we must allow for and follow the path that shows up for us. If that path includes spirituality, that means that you are being shown that spirituality is a way by which you can heal. I absolutely know that you can heal from your childhood pain when you are open to hearing what your inner child has to say. That is what I believe is necessary—we must heal the wounds of our inner child, the one who has been there hurting for long enough. The hurting inner child does not know the hurt you in the present moment. You may be spending a lot of energy not listening to the pain because it hurts too much to touch it. I am telling you, ignoring it is hurting you anyway. It shows up in your life as anxiety, depression, fear, phobias, rage, anger, self-harm, addictions, problematic relationships, issues at work, problems with your child (if you have one), finances, and more.

As you continue reading this book, I invite you to allow yourself to be still and become. To know that this stop on Earth is only temporary. You have been brought here to grow to the next level of mastery within your soul's purpose. To see that there are gifts as well as lessons, and you cannot receive the gift until you have learned the lesson. Sometimes it is a hard lesson, one you would rather turn your back on. If you do that, however, the lesson will continue to show up in other ways until you embrace it. Embrace the lessons, especially the hard and painful ones. You grow when you face them head-on.

Bring it on, because I want you to grow, become, evolve. When we ignore the calling of the pain, we tend to get depressed and anxious. The pain is a portal to growth in order to be, to become. Don't slam the door on your pain, as doing so it is perceived by the deeper mind as a slamming of the door on the soul's yearning to grow.

We think that if we ignore the old stuff, then we are better. We believe that if we push the old stuff down, then it can't hurt us. We hope that now, as an adult, we have risen above all that childhood pain. Guess what? It is still there, and it is affecting you in the present. While I cannot cover each individual source issue of childhood pain in one book, we will look at how healing is possible, no matter the source.

PART 2

WHAT IS SHOWING UP?

CHAPTER 3

Separation from Source

Over the years, I have spent countless hours in meditation. Some of my meditations have been guided by others, some have been experienced in groups, some have been done silently. In whatever manner I have meditated, doing so has always brought me to a place of calm, and many times it has allowed me to gain a deeper understanding of myself and my journey.

I want to take a pause here in order to talk about ego. Many of us have heard the word "ego." Some may have even learned about it for the first time in an Introduction to Psychology class in college. As we go forward together, I want you to understand that the ego I am talking about is not the ego of Western psychology or the one that we normally think of as the "inflated" sense of self.

When I am referring to ego, I am doing so from the perspective of Eastern philosophy. This ego tells us who we are *not* instead of allowing us to own who we are. In Eastern philosophy, the ego is also referred to as the false self, the part of us that develops to protect us from the pain of the reality we are living in. It is the part of us that has been stating all the things we are not. For example: "You are not smart enough, athletic enough, creative enough…" or "You can never earn enough or reach your dreams." These and many other thoughts like them (we all have different ones) are the limiting beliefs we have internalized and come to buy into and own as the truth of who we are.

How does the false self/ego develop? We learn at a young age that we cannot be our true self. That the being who we truly are is not acceptable in the home we are growing up in. Therefore, in order to survive, fit in, and avoid trouble we develop a new way of being. We develop this new way of being to meet the unconscious needs and demands of the people who are raising us. In fact, this new way of being becomes our way of surviving the day-to-day challenges our young self had to cope with when life events were very stressful. A belief forms that says, "If I am this way as opposed to another way, I will be loved, accepted, not yelled at, not punished, seen, heard, and validated."

The young child makes huge, unconscious shifts in who they believe they are in order to survive. These shifts become one's adulthood belief system in terms of who you believe yourself to be. These belief systems are false, but we don't know them as false. The internal dialogue goes something like this: "Life must be this way for me, and it will continue to be this way for me in order for me to continue to be the same person I have always been, the one that my family needs me to be." Were you the scapegoat, protector, rescuer, invisible one, good one, troublemaker, smart one, not enough one? Whatever the answer, we become this identity, we adopt this false belief, and we hold it to be true. We do so because it has kept us alive, so to speak. The problem is, it is *not* true. It is a belief that only developed to protect your very truth, to protect the real and authentic you, to protect the light within that came here to shine. It is up to us to know the wisdom within us, for this is something no one else can teach us. We must be our own guiding light.

Be in abundance. There is more than enough for everyone. Everyone has the potential to tap into the abundance. When you do not feel worthy, you may fill your internal holes with external fillers, and this dulls your light. Some use alcohol, drugs, food, tv, or social media and become numb. You can become so numb, in fact, that you are numb to your own truth.

Once while in meditation, I experienced the following inner knowing:

I made a choice to come into human form, to experience the full expanse of human emotion. To understand the depths of pain and rejoice in the joy. To know what it means to heal; to feel shame, guilt, and emotional conflict. These are feelings that those in human form wish to avoid, yet they are actually the greatest gifts. These are the places where most learning is done. We are not given what we are not ready for. You are given what is needed for you and for your growth. Without first going to the depths of pain, there would be no cry for help. When the ego realizes it is no longer in control, it releases, and you can hear the answers.

CHAPTER 4

Tantrums: A Different Perspective

Without even realizing it, my whole life has been a journey of growth and evolution. For my whole life I've been told about the horrible tantrums I would have as a two-year-old. My mother frequently retold the story of the time when we lived in Brooklyn, NY. I was two years old, and I threw a fit outside of the house and hurled myself down on the sidewalk. She was pregnant with my sister at the time and unable to pick me up. If you have a child and have ever tried to move them when they do not want to be moved, you know it is like trying to lift dead weight.

My father was not home on this day, and she had to ask our neighbor to come lift me off of the sidewalk and bring me into the house. Though I do not recall this experience, I can now have compassion and understanding for that little girl and the emotional pain she was in. I can let her know that she is more than the story of her behaviors because I know she was in pain. As an adult, I had to heal the part of me that held onto the belief that developed out of that story—the belief that my big emotions were too big for others to handle. This was when ego began to develop to protect me and when I began to learn it was not safe to share "big" feelings and fears. Of course, I had no idea I was developing this belief system; it was happening in my subconscious. What I can tell you is that it informed the way I coped with big emotions for the rest of my childhood and into adulthood, until I began doing my own healing work.

I have come to understand that the temper tantrums I had as a two-year-old were not about what was happening in my two-year-old life but were instead tantrums from my inner awareness, my authentic self, my essence, and the pain of realizing that I was being separated from source. The tantrums were my expression of grief and pain. I can now understand that the tantrum was about me being forced to separate from where I came from and forget who I really was. Through meditation, I've been able to remember my soul's journey to the form I am now in. I've been able to remember that it was my choice to be here. During meditation, my two-year-old self remembered where she came from and that she is worthy, loved, seen, and heard. This realization was transformative for me.

I've often thought about two of my own children who, between the ages of eighteen months and three years, began to have tantrums of proportions I had not previously witnessed. When I think back to those very trying times for myself, my husband, and my children, I am filled with sadness because, at the time, I did not understand what their pain was about. Instead, during these knock-down, lengthy tantrums, after my initial compassion wore out (which sometimes happened quite quickly), I would find myself becoming very angry. I can now see and understand that the child having a tantrum is only looking for an abundance of love and compassion. Imagine the shift that could occur if we were able to look at our child who has tantrums as one who is merely looking for love in abundance. In those moments when they feel out of control, they need to know that they are still worthy and deserving of love.

One of the reasons anger sometimes got the better of me when my children would tantrum was that my own repressed anger and sadness from feelings of being separated and alone were being felt somewhere deep inside of me. My own inner child, my two-year-old self, was being activated, and as a result, I at times tantrumed right back at my own children. I did not have the wisdom and understanding I have now; I was a young mom, simply wanting to survive the moment, searching for a way to help my child and myself calm down. I hated how angry I would become, and I knew how out of control it felt at times. I also knew that I didn't know what else to do or how to handle it better, even though I did have an intrinsic knowing that the change had to come from me.

I remember those times in my life with great clarity.

Maybe the remembering is so clear because my children's tantrums were a trigger for my pain, my suffering, my longing to also feel connected. As I now know from my time studying with Dr. Shefali Tsabary, their pain was merely a reflection of my own wounds, wounds that still needed to heal. But, at the time, I remember saying things to myself like, "Why do I have to go through this now?" as if I were the victim of my child's tantrum. That feeling—the feeling of being the victim—was very familiar to me. And we go with what we know. I wish I had the wisdom as a parent and as another human being to understand that their tantrums were really cries of pain. Pain of confusion, of wanting and yet not knowing what the wanting was about. I did not understand at the time that at the age when children come into object permanence, they are also experiencing pain connected to their own separation from source as they used to know it.

Jean Piaget, who developed the theory of object permanence, was a major contributor to the field of psychology. Once object permanence is fully established, a toddler (by the age of eighteen months) is beginning to know that even if something is no longer in sight, it still exists. This is why the game Peek-a-boo is so popular with toddlers—they're not only laughing, they're learning that what goes out of sight still exists. Considering that this awareness is slowly sinking into their consciousness—the awareness that where they came from is still there, but they can no longer return to it--the tantrums make sense to me. These young humans are coming into the realization, on a subconscious level, that they are now here, they are staying, they can no longer go back to where they were, and that is painful, sad, and worth fighting for. It is worth screaming about and asking for someone—anyone—to see, hear, and validate their pain.

What about the kids who don't tantrum? Are they more ready to separate? I have a theory about the children who do not have tantrums. They too chose to come here, but they did not fight the harsh realities they were met with once they arrived. Instead, at a young age, they easily are able to accept that this is where they are right now. They are in the acceptance of the present moment. They are in their being state, able to accept the as-is. They are not in pain from their own separation from source. Instead, they embrace their agreement and do not have the need to fight the process. They are, instead, in flow with the process. They find this flow, this beingness, more easily manageable. They seem to have a more peaceful demeanor. You may even notice that these children who tantrum less or not at all have an easier time playing on their own from a younger age. This solo play helps them integrate their transition from source into human form.

What would have happened if I'd had this wisdom in my early days of parenting? Would I have parented differently? I will never know. What I do know is that I have newfound wisdom and the awareness that I can apply with the intention of helping others as they struggle with similar parenting issues.

CHAPTER 5

You Are a Hidden Treasure

We spend a lot of time wanting to avoid our painful memories. Who wants to go back there, right? It's hard to understand what good it would do to open the book of our life and look back at a past that caused us pain. Have you ever wondered what could be different for you if you allowed yourself to experience your painful feelings, to know them and touch them?

We all are searching to know our purpose here on Earth. Is it possible that the way to uncover this purpose is to go through the healing of your pain? I invite you to not be in fear of the unknown. Instead, step through it boldly and embrace what is being presented to you on the path to healing. It is on the path that you are able to allow the depth of your being to shine through as you grow into the one you were always designed to be.

What we fail to understand is that the pain of our past is the pain of our present. Those old wounds run deep, and if you do not go back and take care of the younger self who was hurt—the hurt inner child—that hurt inner child will continue to run the show. If this is happening in your life, there is a good chance that you find yourself wondering why the same patterns are repeating over and over again. I offer you the following exercise for considering why patterns keep reappearing. Imagine thinking about the challenges we each face along the way. Can you look at each challenge as a wave? As we go through life with its ups and downs, it is like surfing the waves of life. Each wave comes. We either ride it, let it crash over us, or let it take us down. Think about how you have responded to the waves. Is this approach one with which you want to continue to respond? Or, is something bigger calling you to change, to rise up or to rise above.

These are great questions to ask yourself when you are looking at the areas you want to change in your life. Is it time to ask, "What are these waves?" Do the same waves (problems, patterns, themes) come time and time again? Is my response always the same? Do they knock me down, do I ride them, or do I stand up as they crash over me? Does the choice I make depend on the wave? Do I see a pattern in the waves in terms of which ones I can easily ride out and which ones knock me down? Why do I get knocked down? Where is the work I need to do? What do I really need to pay attention to within myself?

I know that's a lot of questions to answer, and I do not

expect you to have the answers to any of them at this point. You are at the starting point of your exploration. It is time to discover what has been happening and what you can do to move from where you are to where you want to be.

Have you ever gone back and looked at what happened to you in your life? Have you been brave enough to face your story? Have you looked at the shame, blame, guilt, embarrassment, fear, shyness, or times when you were bullied, abused, or abandoned (emotionally or physically)? Does the mere reading of those words turn you off? If it does, what that says to me is that the pain is directing the show. The past has the lead role in the performance, and the true you has never had a chance to be the star.

You may feel broken, unloved, unworthy, unlovable, small, not important, angry, or never good enough. Have you ever thought about where these intense feelings come from? Have you ever sat down and really paid attention to them?

Is there a little boy or a little girl hiding in a closet, hoping not to be found because she is so scared about the consequences of being found? And, at the same time, is she also secretly hoping to be found because she wants help? Does this young child just want to know that he matters, that someone misses him or wants to spend time with him?

We all carry our younger selves within us. They hide in the closets of our minds, and I believe that they really want to be found because they are tired of being in pain.

What do you imagine helping them would feel like? Maybe we should start with something easier. How about we just go find him or her.

Take a moment here. Before you read on, close your eyes, and take two or three deep breaths. Once you have done that, imagine, if you will, opening the door and finding that young child hiding inside the closet. He or she may be sitting with knees curled to chest, head down. What is the first thing you would do when you found a child hiding like that alone? Would you crouch down, talk softly, reach out a hand and ask what was wrong? I bet you would.

Let's stop and take a few more breaths. Now, gather up an image of a younger you who is hurting. Imagine that young child who wants and needs help but has no idea how to ask for it. Imagine offering your help. Imagine your adult self, sitting next to that child, just letting that young one know you are there to listen. How would the story play out? Give it a few minutes to unfold; this child may not have ever spoken the words he or she is about to speak. Pause here for as long as you need to.

Once you hear her story, let the child know that she is not alone. That you hear her pain and you are here to help. Even if you don't yet know specifically how you will help, that is okay. Just being there is already assisting. Let the child know that you, the adult, are reading and learning right now about how to help, and you will be with him or her the whole time.

How do you imagine that child would feel after hearing all of this? Would he look up at you? Would she stop crying? Would he or she reach out a hand to be held? Imagine sending this child love. Imagine your heart opening like it would for anyone else in your life that you love, and send love to that child's heart. As that child feels your love, she knows she is not alone and feels relieved to be supported.

Journal Prompts

- What was it like to find the younger version of yourself?

- How did he/she respond to you when you sat down with them?

- What was his or her story?

- What was it like for you to hear the story?

- What was it like to send that little one love?

- How did your young child respond?

You have the power and ability to heal your pain. You have already taken a big step by looking for your inner child and finding him or her. You have already allowed yourself to begin the journey on the path to healing. Be proud of yourself for taking this big first step.

The goal is to heal the pain of the past so it no longer creates pain in your present. You deserve a life full of emotional wholeness, not one riddled with holes of pain. Let's find the hidden treasures that *are* you, residing in you. Let's help you awaken to your true potential and calling.

CHAPTER 6

Feelings, Emotions and Triggers

Whenever people talk about feelings, they often use the word "trigger." What is a trigger? Where do triggers come from? How do you know them? There is so much information out there on this topic that we could read forever and still not have a clear answer to all of our questions or any deeper of an understanding of our emotions than we did when we started looking for answers.

And so I propose, what if it all begins with children's television?

One of the most powerful, easy to access, commonly felt emotions is anger. Everyone knows what anger is. If you say to someone, "I feel angry," they will be able to instantly identify and understand what you mean. If you yell, scream, throw something, or slam on your car horn without saying a word about how you feel, anyone observing you would instantly understand that you were angry.

People think that when they are expressing anger, they are saying how they feel. What if I told you that was not the case? That anger is not so much a feeling as it is a reaction to a feeling. It's a reaction that means that something inside of us was triggered. Once it is triggered, we label the feeling with a commonly understood emotion.

Emotions are reactions to feelings. You see, feelings start on the inside, and emotions are what we show the world. Emotions are our external reactions, and we have many of them. According to Dr. Shefali Tsabary in *The Awakened Family*, "We react with emotion when we are unable to handle our feelings. When we feel uncomfortable, we create a smoke screen of reactivity." She goes on to explain that our behaviors such as eating, drinking, placing blame, and having tantrums are actually smoke screens that feel like feelings but actually represent the avoidance of true feelings. In other words, we can react with the emotions of anger, fear, confusion, frustration, sadness, trepidation, impatience, and even patience and calm to any external stimuli. But while reacting, we may not be accurately giving a voice to what we are *feeling* and *experiencing* on an internal level. Those deeper emotions are not always as easily expressed as anger. Anger can easily be expressed with words or actions, and for most people, anger is readily and easily accessible.

I would like you to think about anger as a character on a children's television show—one who lives in a metal garbage can with a lid that opens quickly and easily. Most of us know this character, and I am sure we can all imagine what that tin can of his looks like. Now, let's think about a scene that is likely to take place on the street where he lives. In this scene, some of the other cute characters are standing outside the garbage can singing a song. Imagine two happy, young characters, one red and one yellow, happily singing the ABCs when all of a sudden, the lid of the garbage can flies open and out pops the green, grouchy character. He was napping and was rudely woken up by all the noise on the sidewalk in front of his home. What is his go-to emotion? Anger. The lid flies open, and out of his mouth comes yelling and aggravation. Maybe he even barks orders at the others, but however he expresses it, the feeling is being expressed through the emotion of anger.

When we are triggered, it is first reflected by the lid of the can flipping open. The emotion of anger is right on top. Anger is easy to access. What happens once the lid explodes and the grouchy character yells at the others? He may calm down because he let off some steam. But, does he take time to look *inside* the can? Does he reflect on his outburst? Does he look inside to explore what caused his explosion, to understand why he "blew his lid?" No, he has no insight. Once he explodes and releases some steam, he feels relief and goes back in his trash can...until the next time he blows the lid off of the can.

Anger is represented by the lid of the can. It is a cover-up emotion, and it keeps everything else pushed down inside. So, the first thing to happen, if we are not in touch with our inner feelings, is anger, and the top flies off the can. Anger takes no effort to get to, no insight, no understanding. It covers up anything that lies underneath. When anger explodes, it does not leave room to look deeper inside to see what might be fueling it. In fact, the angry person may not want to look deeper because, for them, just like the green, grouchy character, being angry is the only response they know. If they give up anger, then what? Who will they be? Would they have to experience other emotions or feel the feelings that are deep inside fueling the anger? Yes, they would. So instead, they stay angry, just like this character stays grouchy.

Now, what about the opposite end of the spectrum? What about the inner feelings that manifest through emotions? Feelings are our internal experiences, the sensations we get inside our body, the things we physically...you guessed it...feel. We feel butterflies in our stomach, we feel our heart race, we feel tears well up in our eyes, we feel tension in our shoulders, tightness in our jaw, clenched fists, shortness of breath. All of these physical sensations are feelings. And when we feel something inside of us, we look to give it a name; when we name it, it becomes an emotion.

The feeling of tears in our eyes can be expressed as sadness, or sometimes, joy. The feeling of butterflies in our stomach might be expressed as nervousness or excitement. The feeling of tension in our jaw or shoulders might be expressed as stress or worry. Do you understand what I am saying? It all begins with a physical feeling, which is then expressed as an emotion. But, the first thing that happens is, we feel something. How many of us are consciously aware of the physical feeling inside before we open our mouth to speak in response? Do you stop, tune in, and look to understand your inner landscape, or do the words and emotions just fly out at whomever is nearby?

If the guy who lives in the garbage can expresses his feelings as the emotion of anger, where do we look to find the true origin of the feelings that lie beneath the lid of that can? To help answer that question, let's meet another character—a cute little furry red guy. When you think of him, what comes to mind? I bet you'd say, "He is talkative, and he expresses his feelings. He will say when he is sad and then also tell you why he is sad. He will say when he is happy and tell you why as well." The difference is, this red character takes the time to look inside. Even when he does get angry, he does not stop there. He reflects and figures out *why* he got angry. Sometimes, he even asks for help from his friends or adults to help him figure it out because he is young and does not yet quite understand all his feelings and emotions. But he knows it is okay to cry, to be frustrated, to be confused, to be irritated, to be stressed, or to be joyful, and he also knows that being tickled is fun. In the end, after he spends time looking inside, figuring out what the physical sensation is that he is experiencing and why that feeling is there, he can express it accurately and appropriately. Once that is completed, he can let it go and go back to being his happy little self, sometimes singing a song. He does not shove the feeling back inside and leave it unattended, just waiting for another reason for it to explode the way the guy who lives in the trash can does.

Feel the feeling but don't become the emotion. Witness it. Allow it. Release it.
—*Crystal Andrus*

It may seem simplistic to think of feelings and emotions in this way—to think of big, overwhelming feelings in terms of characters on a children's television show. But what if you did? What if every time you acted out your feelings, you asked yourself, "Am I the guy in the can or the one who sings about his feelings?" If you are the one in the can, would that bring enough awareness to compel you to stop and check in with your body in order to find the *feeling* causing you to flip your lid? What if you took another moment to acknowledge, "There is some tension in my stomach. I am actually a bit stressed, sad, frustrated, or irritated"? What if you sat with that feeling and that emotion, spoke to someone, or journaled about it until it passed? Would there still be a need for the garbage can lid, or could you allow your inner child to feel better just by paying attention? Maybe that is why the little red guy likes to be tickled—he knows happy feels way more comfortable and fulfilling than upset or angry does.

It is important to remember that all feelings are valid, all emotions are valid. It is up to us to decide how we choose to express them. We get to decide how to show up and how we want to share our inner world and feelings with those in our lives. Ask yourself what will be more pleasant for you: to be living in a garbage can feeling grouchy or singing happy songs, loving to be tickled?

There are no external triggers, even though the guy in the trash can blames everyone else for making him mad. When something is expressed on the outside, what is actually happening is that an internal wound is getting poked. When we say to someone, "You triggered me," in that moment it is up to us to look inside and see what is happening within us that is causing us to suddenly have an internal reaction or physical response to what someone has just said or done or to an event we experience or witness. What we need to start doing more of is owning our reactions and responses.

When you have an experience and get "poked," meaning that you feel it on the inside, it is up to you to own that by saying, "Gee, I just felt something, I wonder what was awakened inside of me?" This then allows us to take ownership of our feelings, emotions, reactions, and responses. It is not someone else's fault if we feel something emotional. Two people can witness the same event at the exact same time and feel two totally different feelings. One may feel joy, while the other feels horror. No one and nothing made each feel the way they felt in relation to what they witnessed. They felt the way they felt, they got "poked" based on what they previously learned in life through their own perceptions of reality.

When I say that nothing on the outside is hurting us, I am not speaking of instances when someone purposefully causes us bodily harm. What I am saying is that, emotionally, no one is hurting us. We are simply feeling our feelings. They are ours. No one else is responsible for what we feel or how we feel it, just as no one is responsible for how we respond to them or heal them. Those actions are up to you, and hopefully it is why you are reading this book, because you are done being "triggered" and "hurt" by others.

At this point it is important to understand the inner child more thoroughly. I have already used the term quite a few times, and before we go further, I want you to have a stronger understanding of who your inner child is. During a meditation I experienced an inner knowing, a wisdom, about the inner child. I feel it is important to share it with you here:

Your inner child is crying to be heard. Reach out to her and let her know you are here. It is here that we know we are not lost or forgotten. The inner child is in need of a healing. This healing comes from hearing the whispers of truth, which arise from your heart, and allowing them to speak. To speak clearly, out loud, to be bold, to be unafraid to let the one inside know she's not forgotten. The one who must always remember her is you. The one who sits and waits to be seen must be remembered by you. Make space for her, make space for the pain, the truth, the light. You see, the pain of the memories cannot do more harm than the pain of the original event. By not addressing the pain of the child who lived through the event, you keep the pain alive and the wounds open. The wounds seep toxins into every area of your life--into all relationships, spouses, friends, parents, children, colleagues. Everywhere is touched by unhealed pain, but you are so unaware of that. What goes wrong is going wrong because of pain from the past. It just keeps repeating, and you do not shift; maybe blame is placed outside of you onto others or other situations. Unhealed toxic pain is damaging. The inner child cries for you to see her, hold her, love her. The adult self re-parents her own inner child from an aligned and healed way, and when she does, the pain of her past cannot spill onto the child in their present.

After gleaning that, I realized, *Holy shit, this is the truth and I cannot ignore it anymore.* Ignoring oneself only pushes the pain deeper into each of our cells. This is why unhealed toxic pain is damaging. The question then becomes, *How do we heal this unhealed toxic pain?* I've asked myself this question over and over again.

First, we need to recognize that there is a part of us that is looking to heal. Since you've made it this far, I am going to assume you are in agreement with this basic principle. That part that needs to heal is, I believe, your inner child, which shows itself through the voice you hear in your head as you move through your day—the voice of fear, doubt, worry, lack. This voice may say things like, "Do you really need this? "You don't deserve this." "You are not important." "I am afraid to (fill in the blank)." "I can't." This is the voice of your pain. Your inner child is in pain and is calling out to you, the adult, for help. For you to see her. To let her know she is heard. To let him know he is important. To let her know she is worthy. To let him know he is valuable.

Once we can recognize this voice, we become conscious of it when it shows up. It's as if you are hearing a new friend who needs help. In order to heal some part of the self, we must first see that it is there. We must be able to step to the side, observe the self, look inside, and say, "Hi, I see you." This may feel really scary; that is normal. New things are often not easy, and emotionally scary things aren't typically approached with excitement and anticipation. Instead, they're most often met with fear, trepidation, and resistance.

The injured inner child is the one who holds onto the pain, who holds onto the stories, who is afraid to let them go. The false self/ego holds onto the conclusions that were reached about the self, based on the stories you have come to believe are true. A story develops, a story of the ignored child, the not-enough child, the I-am-not-important child, the I-am-invisible child. The false self then identifies with the conclusions drawn, based on the story. These conclusions may resemble "I am no good," "I deserve it," "I am worthless," "I am invisible," "My feelings don't matter or count," "I don't matter," "I am not important," "This is not my body," "I can't have my own thoughts or feelings," "I am not lovable," or "I am not enough." When we are triggered, it is the inner child who gets woken up. It is his or her pain that is getting your attention in the now.

I want to offer you another way to understand triggers, our emotional pain points, from a framework I like to call The Container. Within each of us is a container that serves as a safe holding space for our pain. This container is opened when you hear your child's or loved one's emotional pain. We cannot call their pain a trigger, as doing so would suggest that they were given responsibility for our emotions and reactions. Instead, they are our awakeners. There are no external triggers, only internal wounds. Your pain is awakened, the lid of your container gets flipped, and you can see inside. Once that pain is awakened, it is your responsibility to take care of yourself. It is your job to be aware and not project it out onto another or become reactive and blame someone else.

What really is happening is, one's current emotional pain is very similar to that of the inner child of the person with whom they are engaging. Your inner child intimately knows the feeling or experience the other person is sharing. If they are expressing hopelessness, sadness, unworthiness, embarrassment, frustration, or confusion, and we too know those feelings (and they have not been healed), we may react from the place within the container where our *own* inner child has stored these same or similar unhealed emotions. We know these feelings and emotions in the present, but more significantly we know them from the past. If you were to react, you would be reacting from a place of pain that is anchored in *your* past.

For example, if I am listening to my child or spouse

share something painful, the lid on my container is flipped. My inner child gets woken up if I am unaware or unconscious of this, and I may find myself getting mad, impatient, closing down, exploding, or having any other number of knee-jerk reactions. Why does this happen? Because their pain is so close to mine. And, if I had never spent time healing that wounded inner child, my inner child, my younger self will react to the child or loved one in front of me. The real question is, how do we make it stop?

The goal is to take a pause and look inside at where in your body you just had a physical reaction to the external stimuli. We will learn about the chakras shortly, and once you further understand that concept, you will be able to identify which chakra is holding the pain that has been woken up. This identification is the first step.

We identify the chakra by taking a pause. This can take time. Do not be fooled into believing that you can pause for just one moment and fix everything. Pausing in the moment is merely the first step, and it will help prevent the knee-jerk reaction that has been your pattern.

When this happens, take a moment and feel where you were just poked. Was it your stomach, your throat, your heart? Did you get a headache? The body will and does give you clues to where you are storing blocked emotions. You want to begin to become aware of your body's sensations so that you can begin to ask yourself, "What is this about?" and "Where is this coming up in my body?" It is at this point that we can begin to spend more time taking care of our feelings. It takes time to sort through them, to deconstruct patterns, to understand the "why" of them. But this is also when you begin to have insights and can use journaling and meditation to explore the pain and understand both yourself and your unmet needs, the ones that show up as pain and are acted out through reactions.

All of the experiences we have ever had in our lives are stored in our deeper minds. Most, if not all, experiences have some kind of emotional reaction attached to them, ranging from joy to despair. It's important to remember that the deeper mind has no sense of time. So, if you learned a coping skill when you were five years old and got hurt but weren't comforted, then now, when you get hurt at the age of thirty, you likely use the same coping skill you used as a five-year-old. And you do so without even realizing where it came from. This happens because the deeper mind knows the feeling and emotion, and when that particular feeling and resulting emotion come up, the deeper mind reacts with its original coping skills. Those coping skills were effective when you were five, but they probably aren't when you're thirty. I don't know about you, but I certainly do not want my five-year-old self running the show of my fifty(plus)-year-old self!

The way to help yourself heal from the emotional injuries is to go inside your body and listen to the clues it gives you. From here, we can connect those clues to the chakras. Once you understand the basic traits of each chakra, you will get even more clues as to what is going on within you. It is like becoming your own detective with a map to follow. We can take it a step further in hypnosis and actually talk to the inner child, hear her stories, her thoughts, her beliefs, and the impact that those thoughts and beliefs have on her as an adult. Once we know all this, we can do a healing with the inner child through a process of transformational hypnosis, by accessing the wisdom and knowing of your deeper mind and your higher self.

Ways to take care of your emotions when you are in pain

- Ask yourself, what kind of pain am I in?
- Use kind words with yourself and eliminate harsh, critical judgments.
- Feel the feelings.
- Acknowledge the pain for what it is in the moment.
- Have patience with yourself.
- Meditate.

CHAPTER 7

Knowing and Trusting in Self

What does it mean to trust in the whole? In short, it means that all you need is within you. Trust in the knowing that is in your soul—the part that holds you together, the part that responds when something feels "right" or "off." Trust in yourself, for you really do know all you need to know and all you are called forth to follow.

We cannot truly know another until we know our self. We cannot know the outside until we know the inside. We learn about our outer world, the world around us, by taking it in and holding it up like a mirror against what we know or believe to be true. It is important to learn how to trust our own internal measuring stick, because if we cannot, how can we know what is true for us? We develop this knowing by listening to what rings true in our heart. You must feel love already inside yourself. You must have what you know to be true to the self in order to know it and feel it. We know the feeling of truth in the body because we have a physical response. When I feel my truth, I get warm and tingly, or I feel chills run through me from head to toe. How do you get validation when something "rings" true for you? Take a moment to think about it.

Trusting yourself is a crucial part of healing. There is a place within where you can go to find trust in the self. This place is like a garden; a place to find inner wisdom, inner knowing, and inner truth. When you trust in yourself, wholly and fully, you can allow life to unfold for you. You get to step forward, not in fear but with confidence. When you trust yourself, you are saying to your heart, "I trust you." When you block this energy, the energy of trust that emanates from your heart, you are blocking the unfolding of all that is possible for you. You block not only the not-so-good but also the good.

When I meditate, I open myself up to receive messages for my highest and greatest good. This action reflects a deep commitment to trusting myself. I make sure I am grounded. When I am grounded and I enter this energetic space, I am fully trusting myself and whatever I experience. I trust that the messages I hear are there for me, to help me, to offer guidance, or to enable me to help others. Sometimes I go into meditation and hear nothing; there is only silence. In those meditations, I trust that what I needed that day wasn't a particular message, but instead, simply the quiet.

Can you begin to trust that everything you need in order to heal, feel better, and grow is already inside of you?

That your soul arrived here as perfect? There is an inner knowing that you possess and have the ability to tap into that will allow you to reach your goals and heal if you let yourself go there. Trusting yourself is trusting your heart. It is trusting that intuitive knowing that does not come from a place of fear but of self-love. Trusting yourself means knowing yourself and having confidence in that knowing.

Your truth cannot be dependent upon the stories that others hold about you. Your inner truth must have somewhere to stick within you. This is where trust comes in. Trust in the knowing that you can rely on you. When you are solid and grounded in the truth of who you are, in your ability to know and trust your own heart, your emotional energy will not fall prey to false attraction. It will repel any beliefs that you can fix the inside by fixing the outside. If you believe that feeling better internally is dependent on what and who is outside of you, you are working too hard. That approach is like climbing up a hill while carrying a lot of extra weight on your back. When we do this, we are actually projecting a false outer self. Doing this takes far more work and emotional energy to keep in place, as it is fueled by the fear that it will be found out, and then you, your self, will be left holding the costume while the empty shell is right back at the beginning trying to figure out another way to survive. But in truth, the way is not to simply survive. It is to do the deep healing you were called here to do. The goal is to thrive.

I believe we are all abundant, healing energy, and this

energy resides within each one of us. It is up to you to tap into your own infinite potential as you heal your own heart. In order to truly get to know yourself, a process of healing needs to take place. As you heal, you will get to know yourself and understand yourself in new ways and with new insights. This has the potential to open you up to new possibilities. Healing involves arriving with an open, uninhibited heart. Healing involves a rising from within, an awareness that you must be responsible for taking care of yourself. It is within us that all the gifts to heal reside. Do the inner work of self-exploration. Healing is brave work, and it is also incredibly transformative. It will bring you to exactly where you need to be until you are ready to do more healing. The more you learn to tune in and understand yourself, the more you will be able to continue to do so on an even deeper level. It is a practice that, over time, becomes a new way of being.

Healing is a process of sifting through the layers of pain bodies within us and addressing the hurt with the intention to help the hurt transform. We want it to transform from a place of pain to a place that is loved, a place that can feel the love. In the end, isn't that what all of us want? To be loved? To be able to love ourselves? To know we are loved by others?

There is no shame in the knowing of the truth. We all must know our own internal truths. It is okay to look at them, own them, and share them. The more we share the most painful parts of ourselves, the more deeply we heal the wounds, for we allow those deep emotional wounds to heal from the inside out. Healing is the way to wholeness and health. You cannot heal only on the surface. When you do, the pain gets acted out anyway. The ego will sabotage, and the thinking mind will be in charge, allowing all of the old tapes with the old beliefs to emerge and play. The knowing of the soul will find peace in the healing of the heart.

There is a place of stillness within the very center of your being. When you can access this place of stillness, all forms of the self that are in pain will simply fall away. You will then realize that the pain is no longer necessary. It is not up to us to define ourselves based on the definitions of those around us; others' definitions are coming from their own judgements. Those judgements actually arise from a place of pain within the other person, from their own unhealed inner child and pain-body.

In his book, *A New Earth*, Eckhart Tolle defines the pain-body as "an accumulation of old emotional pain" (p.140) He also writes, "The energy field of old but still very much alive human emotion that lives in almost every human being is the pain-body" (p.142). He states that it is human tendency to perpetuate old emotions, and almost all of us carry these old emotions in our energy field. Therefore, it is up to each one of us to learn to be present in each moment and not define our self purely based on the old emotional pain we carry around.

The only way to truly know one's self is to step away from identifying it via definition and simply step into acceptance of it. It is important to make this shift, because definition comes from society. Definition represents something on the outside that we were taught we had to be in order to fit in, to survive, to be successful. Definition is, in truth, based in fear. We have bought into the definition that a good student gets A's and B's in school. A successful person earns a certain amount of money. A successful relationship is to be married. We have come to believe that if we are not these things, if we do not fit these definitions, we are somehow wrong, less than, bad, not worthy, unlovable.

The goal is to be part of the free-flowing energy of experiences that are here for you to enjoy. To make your own path to success and health, not based on what society says you should do or be, but instead based on what you know to be true for you. A truth that echoes back to you the free-flowing energy of your very own soul. You came here with a special purpose. You get to create an Earthly vision around your purpose and find your unique way to live it.

Living your purpose is the path to healing and wholeness. It is up to you honor what is innate within you and listen to your internal knowing rather than the voice of others. When you tune in and listen to your essence, your true self, you will find yourself on the path of your life's purpose. It is being on this path, moment by moment, which offers us opportunities to heal. Any time we wish we were on another's path, doing it their way and looking to have their results, we find ourselves walking in a circle without a destination because the path we are seeking is not ours but another's.

You were born with special gifts. In fact, your gifts are so special and so unique that no one else has exactly the gifts that you have. As you continue on your journey of getting to know who you are, it is as if you are slowly opening the wrapping paper that protectively covers these gifts. You are the one who will carefully remove the tape, peel back the layers of paper, and open your box. When you look inside, you will receive the gifts contained therein, those knowings, those truths that are singularly unique to you. Your job is to do you, to honor you, to be in the beautiful experience of *being* you.

Maybe part of your path to your purpose involves sitting quietly in nature and watching the butterflies dance, being present with the birds as they soar and glide overhead. To sway in the breeze with the leaves on the treetops. To feel the sun on your face and the breeze on your skin as you float, adrift on the peaceful waters of inner and outer harmony. To be like the bass and treble clef scales, working in perfect harmony to make beautiful music. When your internal state matches your external reality, you too will be in harmony, making your own heart sing with the beautiful music that rises up from within you and only you.

We all have the ability to float on the place of the formless, on the place of trust, in the place of peace and inner knowing that right here, right now is just perfect, designed for us to grow, heal, learn, and love. This place of quiet within is where healing starts. We must tap into the quiet, feel the quiet, and trust that in the quiet we can heal. In order to heal, we must first be able to feel. In order to feel, we are called to go to a quiet place within the center of our stillness, and with our inner awareness, allow ourselves to pull back the curtains that have protected us from pain. To look at the part of us that needs its feelings recognized, seen, heard, acknowledged, and allowed. To connect with the one inside who went into hiding a long time ago (or maybe just yesterday) and is now asking you for help to begin the journey toward healing.

What are the steps? What do we need to first understand? We want to be able to say, "I am healed, I feel better." We want to feel better when we look at that specific part of our story, to be able to look at it without attachment, without pain, without flashbacks.

Now, pull back the curtain that you hide behind. Allow your imagination to get a picture, an image, an idea of who the one behind that curtain looks like. Let's look at that one's feelings. We know she is in pain, or we would not have found her hiding behind the curtain. Are you ready to look at the pain? To feel the pain? Are you ready to allow it to pass through you and then release it out of you? If you are, you are ready for the next step. If you are not, that is okay too. Please read the following section to discover whether or not you are ready.

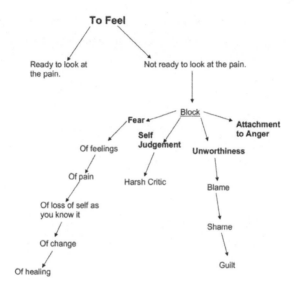

First, make the choice to state:

I am not ready yet **or** *I am ready to look at the pain.*

I AM NOT YET READY TO LOOK AT MY PAIN

If you are feeling that you are not yet ready, you need to take some quiet time to explore why. There can be a multitude of reasons for your unreadiness. Do not sit in judgement of yourself. Simply accept that, for right now, this is the way it is. This is how you are feeling; be with that.

I invite you, before you go forward, to take some time to write down your responses to the following prompts:

Ask yourself, *Am I afraid to feel these feelings?*

If so, go deeper, and ask yourself, *Afraid of what exactly?*

Are you afraid that you will get upset, cry, have to remember things you don't want to?

Are you afraid you will be angry at yourself or others?

Are you afraid you won't know what to do once you look at it, or that are there other reasons for the fear?

Is there anything else there besides fear?

Is your critical or judgmental self is coming in and asking, *What for?* when it comes to wanting to address this. What is the negative self-talk you are hearing?

Are there feelings of loneliness coming up? Feelings that you do not deserve to feel better? Are you entertaining thoughts that feeling better is so foreign to you that you just can't?

Are you attached to your anger? Are you concerned that, without your anger, you won't know who you are? Does a piece of you like being angry, because when you are angry it is such a big feeling that you do not have space to feel anything else?

Do you not feel worthy of healing? Have you felt unworthy of what life has to offer you for so long that you ask yourself, *How can I be worth healing?*

Do you question whether or not you are important enough to anyone else? My question to you is, are you important to *yourself*?

Since you have gotten this far, I have to assume the answer to this question is yes. You are important enough to yourself because you are reading a book on how to heal. And, if you can read a book on how to heal, there must be a part of you, somewhere deep inside, that believes you can. A part that got your attention and brought that attention to this book as you were searching.

I am here to tell you that you *are* important, worthy, brave enough, and ready to touch what has made you angry or upset. This is not a place for self judgement; this is a place for self-acceptance. Welcome to this place of accepting that this is where you are, right here and right now, on the precipice of change, honesty, and hope that the next moment will just be a little better than the one that just passed.

Take a look at the chart above (page 101) in which I break down what might be happening if you are in the place of are not yet being ready to feel the pain. If you are not ready to feel the pain, that tells me there may be blocks inside that are getting in the way of your ability to access those parts of you. The four primary such emotional blocks are fear, self-judgement, unworthiness, and attachment to anger.

Fear

Let's first look at fear. It is easy to say, "I am afraid," but have you looked at possible reasons why? Are you afraid of your feelings? Of your pain? Are you afraid that you will lose yourself as you are now? Are you afraid of change or that you might have to change? Are you afraid to heal because maybe you don't understand what that means or what it could look like?

Self-Judgement

The next emotional block is self-judgement. Do you have a harsh internal critic or judge who is always telling you that you are wrong? Does this critic wag his or her finger in your face, throwing "should haves" at you? When you hear those "should haves," do you back down and retreat? Do you question who you are and why you are doing this? Do you tell yourself you are just not worth it?

Unworthiness

The third emotional block is unworthiness. Have you ever considered the feelings and experiences that underpin the feelings and emotions of unworthiness? These can be some of the most powerful emotions, ones that stop us in our tracks. These are the emotions of blame, shame, and guilt. Where have they come from, and what do you need to understand about yourself and each of these emotions in order to move through them?

Attachment to Anger

The fourth emotional block is attachment to anger. Are you attached to anger? Do you believe that the anger helps you? Does it somehow serve a purpose in your life? How long has the anger been there? If you do not know, have you ever explored why it showed up and why it stayed?

These are all questions to ask yourself. I invite you to take some time and explore each of the blocks. Sit with each one, journal about it, determine which ones resonate with you. Take some time to get to know yourself. This is how we heal--by becoming more and more comfortable in the emotional skin we live in.

Follow the journal prompts starting back on page 102 to explore your possible emotional blocks to healing as they are related to fear, self-judgement, unworthiness, and attachment to anger.

Who *am I without my pain?* Let's take another moment and ask ourselves once again, *Am I ready to look at the pain?* After taking the time to journal about each of the emotional blocks, I am hopeful that you are even more ready. Remember, you are exactly where you need to be.

I AM READY TO LOOK AT MY PAIN

I am glad to see you here. It is a brave place to be. Give yourself credit for showing up, for doing the work in the above section, for being committed to healing and growing. After all, this is about you, no one else.

Being ready means that you have a basic understanding of an aspect or aspects of yourself that have been causing you enough pain in your life that you are ready to look at them. It means that your emotional pain is actually making you uncomfortable. It is exactly the space I was in when I made that call to a therapist while in graduate school. I know it is scary, and I know it feels vulnerable. In my opinion, there is no braver place to be than standing in your vulnerability, asking for help, and being open enough to receive it.

As we move along, the word we need to more fully understand is vulnerability. The foremost expert in vulnerability is Brene Brown, Ph.D., L.M.S.W. If you have not read her books or watched her YouTube videos, I encourage you to do so. She offers a deep dive into vulnerability-- how to understand it, break it down, and get yourself out of it. While I obviously cannot recount the content of her books, I do want to share her definition of vulnerability and some of her thoughts surrounding it so that you have a basic understanding in order to move forward with your own learning, healing, and growth. In order to move forward, we must first understand where we currently are, because the place to start is wherever you are in the current moment.

Brené defines vulnerability as "uncertainty, risk, and emotional exposure." She explains that vulnerability is at the core of all of our emotions and feelings. Just to feel is to be vulnerable. If we believe that vulnerability is a weakness, we must conclude that to feel is a weakness (*Daring Greatly*, pp.33,34). She goes on to share that "Vulnerability is the birthplace of love, belonging, joy, courage, empathy, and creativity. It is the source of hope, empathy, accountability, and authenticity." (*Daring Greatly* p.34). To me, the space of vulnerability is the bravest space you can experience.

When we decide to share something that feels shameful and puts us in the emotional space of vulnerability, we must be clear as to our intention for sharing. When we share shame, we need to be clear that it is being shared in a safe space and that the sharing is for our own healing.

When you share shame and allow yourself to sit in the seat of vulnerability, you are actually doing very deep self-care. Sharing with the intention to heal with safe people allows you to also feel safe in the powerful experience of being vulnerable. Feeling safe in vulnerability is empowering. The converse is also true: to share shame with those who are not safe and do not honor you can place you in a disempowered space of vulnerability. It can lead to the feeling or inner experience of revictimization of the shame, and this is not healing. Instead, you only create another level of pain to sort through when you journey back onto the path of healing. Be aware, be awake, and be conscious to your shares. Above all else, be sure you are honoring yourself. No one else will take better care of you than you will.

There is no rejection when we share our truth with someone. When we are brave enough, when we "enter the arena and Dare Greatly" as Brené Brown writes, we step into our true self, we call upon our higher self, and we speak the truth of our hearts. We speak our vulnerabilities and ask the one we share with to hold our heart gently, with care, and with the same love with which they hold their own heart. If they reject what we share, we need to be in the awareness that they are not rejecting us or denying our truth but instead rejecting the truth within *them* as we shine light to a story, situation, or memory. The rejection is not a rejection of the self but their rejection of the piece of them that resonates with the universal truth of what we've shared.

You cannot hold onto shame. Shame keeps you stuck and feeling overly responsible to that which is not yours. It is a burden placed on your back that you have kept and continue to carry. It causes internal damage to your body, mind, and spirit. Healing must occur. Before you can speak your truth to another, you must first speak the truth to yourself. You must do your own inner work and healing. You cannot speak your truth if it is damaged by shame, blame, or guilt. You can only speak your truth from a healthy inner landscape. Once healthy and clear, another's response cannot damage you, and you can share your truth from a place of wholeness and self-compassion. This is a great gift you give yourself, and it is part of the Spiral of Healing.

CHAPTER 8

The Chakra System: A Brief Overview

It's now time to explore the chakra system. As a practicing master An-Ra energy healer and hypnotherapist I believe—and I have confirmed through my work with clients—that healing needs to happen in our bodies at a cellular level. When we get in touch with our wounded inner child, we must also be aware of *where* we feel emotional hurts in our physical bodies. Every experience we have ever had is stored in our cellular memory. Just as we have muscle memory, we have cellular memory. One way to tap into and heal at a cellular level is through the chakras.

I will explain the seven major chakras, but please understand that this is only a brief overview. If you feel called to take a deeper dive into learning about the chakras, there are many great books and references. All you need to do is type the word chakra into your search engine and *voila*, you will get more suggestions than you could possibly read during this lifetime. However, if you are looking for a place to start, I would recommend both Barbara Brennan's and Anodea Judith's work.

Barbara Brennan is the author of *Hands of Light, A Guide to Healing in the Human Energy Field*, which was written in 1987. When this book was written, energy healing was not something talked about by "everyday" people as commonly as it is today. These concepts, which are so beautifully expressed in her book, were both groundbreaking and validating to those who were, at the time, practicing healing energy work. Today, if you mention Reiki to someone, even if they don't know exactly what it is, chances are they have heard of it. An-Ra, like Reiki, is a system of energetic healing conducted through the chakra system.

Barbara Brennan and her book stand out because she is scientifically trained as both a physicist and a psychotherapist. She was a research scientist at NASA. She approaches the chakra system and its vast ability to help us heal at the physical, emotional, and metaphysical level. If you are looking for proof that the chakra system and energetic healing are real and possible, I encourage you to explore her book. Open your heart and mind to the concepts, and understand that, as you tap into the energy within us and surrounding us (our aura), you can heal.

As human beings, we each have seven major chakras. Chakras are our body's major energy centers. You may have heard them referred to as qi (or chi), which is usually translated as "vital life force." According to Chinese philosophy, qi is the force that makes up and binds together all things in the universe. It is, paradoxically, both everything and nothing.

In acupuncture, the energy system in the body is referred to as chi. The chakras reside in our energy field, and it is the energy that connects our inner and outer worlds. The energy field of the chakras extend out to a distance of about two inches both in front of and behind your physical body. They run through your body front to back, like a funnel with the narrow end in the center and the wide-open end outside of the physical body. Through the open end, we pick up on the energy around us and take it in.

I will go through each of the seven chakras so that you know their names, where they are located in the body, and what each is responsible for. Each chakra has a positive aspect as well as the opposite. I do not like to think of any aspect of the chakras as negative, because if there is a block, unhealthy thought body, or emotional pain present, I see that as my teacher. In fact, when working with clients I am actually *looking* for the blocks, the points where the chakra feels stuck, thick, sluggish, hot, or cold. These are all clues that there is some part of that chakra that needs to heal. This is where I tune in with my client and where we begin to look inside for the underlying reason behind the blocked or sluggish chakra. I use what I find, especially those things we would traditionally label as "bad" or "not good" as a teacher for me when I am working with someone, even if that someone is myself.

Chakras can be opened or closed at any given time.

They usually spin energetically in a clockwise motion. You can clear a chakra and have it open, but then have an experience or a strong emotion from which that chakra may begin to shut down or again become blocked. Let's use the example of driving, when you suddenly need to slam on your breaks. What emotion sets in? Fear. The thought that shows up may be, *I could have died or gotten hurt. My safety was threatened.* When we have a close call like that, the root chakra will get blocked, because that is the chakra associated with day-to-day life and death issues in our humanity. It will take time to recover from that shock of a near miss before the root chakra can again open.

The beautiful thing to remember here is that within ourselves, we have the ability to heal and clear chakras as needed. They do not have to stay blocked, but throughout the course of the day our energy centers are opening and closing based on our emotional and physical life experiences. Unless you know about your chakras, are aware of them, and are in tune with your body and these energy centers, you will have no idea that this is happening, yet it is. It is just like our hearts beating and our lungs breathing. It is happening without conscious awareness. When you stop and pay attention, you become aware of your breath moving in and out of your lungs and body. If you really quiet your mind and sit still, you can also tune in and feel your heart beating. My hope for you is that you will be able to learn to be in quiet within yourself, so that you can be in touch with your body and the chakras to help you in your healing, growth, and becoming.

Another benefit that comes from having an awareness of the chakra system is, you will not find yourself stuck as often, and when you do get emotionally or energetically stuck, you will have the necessary tools to get yourself unstuck more quickly and more easily.

Below is a diagram for you to refer to in order to help you better understand where each of the chakras is located. Each can give us much information. In addition to each chakra being energetically located at a certain point in our body and holding specific emotions, it is also connected to the physical organs in that part of our body. Each chakra is as aspect of your consciousness. They each have their own color. If a woman comes to me with infertility challenges, which is one of my areas of expertise, I know there are probably emotional issues going on in the spleen chakra, because that is where her reproductive organs are.

I will now further explain each chakra and talk a bit about its location and emotional aspects.

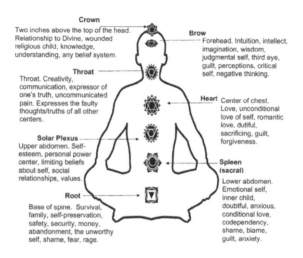

Crown
Two inches above the top of the head. Relationship to Divine, wounded religious child, knowledge, understanding, any belief system.

Brow
Forehead. Intuition, intellect, imagination, wisdom, judgmental self, third eye, guilt, perceptions, critical self, negative thinking.

Throat
Throat. Creativity, communication, expressor of one's truth, uncommunicated pain. Expresses the faulty thoughts/truths of all other centers.

Heart Center of chest. Love, unconditional love of self, romantic love, dutiful, sacrificing, guilt, forgiveness.

Solar Plexus
Upper abdomen. Self-esteem, personal power center, limiting beliefs about self, social relationships, values.

Spleen (sacral)
Lower abdomen. Emotional self, inner child, doubtful, anxious, conditional love, codependency, shame, blame, guilt, anxiety.

Root
Base of spine. Survival, family, self-preservation, safety, security, money, abandonment, the unworthy self, shame, fear, rage.

Root Chakra

Location: Base of the spine.

Color: Red

Issues and feelings: Survival, family, self-preservation, safety, security, money, abandonment, the unworthy self, shame, fear, rage.

Physical Organs: Hips, lower spine, male/female external sex organs, legs, feet, coccyx, rectum, sciatic nerve.

Spleen Chakra (also called sacral)

Location: Lower abdomen (about 2 inches below the belly button)

Color: Orange

Issues and feelings: Emotional self, creativity, relationship/sexual issues, sexuality, inner child, emotionally charged thoughts, fear, power, doubtful, anxious, disappointed, conditional love, codependency, shame, blame, guilt, anxiety.

Physical Organs: Female reproductive organs, bladder, bowel, lower back, lower intestines, prostate.

Solar Plexus Chakra

Location: Upper abdomen. (between the rib cage and diaphragm)

Color: Yellow

Issues and feelings: Self-esteem, personal power center, limiting beliefs about self, materialism, manipulating/controlling self, helpless, will, social relationships, work, drive, values.

Physical Organs: Liver, upper intestines, stomach, gallbladder, pancreas, diaphragm, lower lungs, kidneys.

Heart Chakra

Location: Center of chest.

Color: Green

Issues and feelings: Love, unconditional love of self, emotions, kindness, forgiveness, sadness, suffering, romantic love, dutiful, moral dilemmas, sacrificing, guilt, vulnerability.

Physical Organs: Heart, lungs, circulatory system, thymus gland, entire immune system.

Throat Chakra

Location: Throat.

Color: Blue

Issues and feelings: Creativity, communication, expressor, expression of one's truth, will, choice, manipulative, uncommunicated pain, lying. Expresses the faulty thoughts of all the other centers.

Physical Organs: Throat, neck, shoulders, arms, hands, fingers, mouth, teeth, tongue, jaw, esophagus, thyroid, parathyroid, upper respiratory system, vocal cords.

Brow Chakra

Location: Forehead (sometimes referred to as the "third eye")

Color: Purple

Issues and feelings: Intuition, intellect, imagination, fantasy, wisdom, judgmental self, guilt, perceptions, insights, visualizations, critical self, ridged or negative thinking, the senses.

Physical Organs: Head, mind, scalp, ears, eyes, pituitary gland, endocrine system, immune system, brain function, sinus.

Crown Chakra

Location: Two inches above the top of the head.

Color: Violet (light purple)

Issues and feelings: Relationship to the Divine, wisdom, wounded religious child, knowledge, understanding, any belief system. If blocked, it interferes with the connection to source energy, not being spiritually aware.

Physical Organs: Central nervous system, skeletal system, spinal cord, brain stem, and pineal gland.

I hope that, as you continue to read and work through the journal prompts, you will refer back to this chakra chapter. One purpose in understanding your chakras is gaining a better understanding of yourself, your emotional responses, and how your physical body reacts to and possibly holds onto emotions. Understanding your energetic system is a key component to understanding yourself, and it is part of the path to embracing yourself as well as finding emotional health, balance, and healing.

CHAPTER 9

The Purposeful Pause

It is time to start exploring how to move from reacting to responding with a goal of being as present as possible as well as being connected to yourself and in tune with the feelings you are experiencing in each moment. The idea is to *not* get stuck in the story you are telling yourself. The reason we incorporate storytelling is, we're looking for a way to feel better in the moment. However, that does not work, because when you begin to story tell, rationalize, or make excuses for yourself or another, you are not in the moment. You are lost in thought, somewhere in the future or the past. And guess what? That is not being present.

When I was employed as a social worker at the nursing home, I worked very closely with the Rabbi, as we were both consistently counseling residents and family members. While he and I were in the lobby one day speaking with a resident who was stuck in a lot of worry about her future, he told her something that I have kept with me all of these years. I have no idea where he got it, but here it is.

"Yesterday is done, tomorrow has not happened yet, today is the present and the present is a gift."

When he shared this with our resident, she stopped. It made her pause long enough to truly be in that moment. It did not take her worry away; at her age, that wasn't our goal. But, if even for a few minutes she could get relief from her incessant worry, we were successful in helping to alleviate even just a bit of her suffering.

The present is the gift that is here for all of us at all times. Our breath is another gift that is here for all of us at all times. Do you recognize these gifts? Do you sit in awareness of the gifts of the present moment and your breath? Do you even realize that both are happening right now as you read these words? Because they are. It is a beautiful thing to realize that these two precious gifts are always here for you. All that is required to receive them is that you bring your awareness to them.

Have you ever taken a hike in the woods or gone to a large amusement park and suddenly realized you couldn't figure out where you were? If so, what was the next thing you did? You probably looked for a map. And, when you found the map, you looked for the big (red) arrow that's pointing to the spot where you're standing alongside the words "You are here." This is what I want you to begin to think about when you are being present—that you are at the spot on the map, right where the arrow is pointing, noting that You Are Here. In being here, you now know exactly where you are: standing here, breathing, aware of yourself in this very moment, being still.

There is a stillness that comes with being present, that comes with being in quiet with yourself and being comfortable in the stillness. Sometimes we don't know how to tolerate the stillness, and sometimes we don't want to, usually because when we are still, we begin to feel things, maybe even uncomfortable things like anxiety. It is at that point when we become aware of a feeling of discomfort. We may feel guilt, fear, regret, or sadness. We work so hard to avoid feelings and emotions that we rarely sit still. Can you relate to this?

What does it mean to "be present?" What does "being present" look like? Being present means showing up in each moment, fully and completely. It means embodying that moment. It means being in the moment, the one you are in right now, right here. When you realize that you are no longer in the moment, that thought alone brings you back to the moment. When you are in each moment, you cannot be anywhere else. You accept the fact that You. Are. Here. You really can't be anywhere else, right? In the next moment, maybe you will move, but in this one you are in life as it is showing up for you. You may fool yourself into believing that you are experiencing each moment, but I challenge you to ask yourself, *Am I really? Am I really allowing myself to experience, to be in, each moment?*

Do you ever find yourself feeling anxious? Do your

thoughts wander? Do you find yourself thinking about the next day, your trip next month, or what you can next post on Facebook? Or, are you lamenting yesterday? Kicking yourself for handling a life event in one way and not the other? Are you worrying about what was not done? Are you thinking about an argument you had, or remembering an event that you attended where you had a lot of fun? Do you find yourself in the past, living in those memories, good or bad? This is actually what most of us do from moment to moment, hour to hour, day to day, week to week, month to month, and year to year. And then we get into conversations with friends and profess, "Wow, this day/week/month/year went so fast. Where did the time go? I can't believe it is a new year already." Have you had this experience?

When you are in worry about yesterday or tomorrow, you are not here. The map does not say, "You *will be* here, just walk ten more steps." It also does not say, "You were just over there, so go back ten steps." It sort of reminds me of the game "Mother May I" that we played when I was little. In case you never played it, the goal is to race to get to the person who is "it." You don't want to stay still, you want to be given permission by the "it" person to move forward, not back. You do not want to be where you are because you want to win, believing that feeling good will come from what is going to happen next (if you win), instead of realizing that staying just where you are means that for right now, you are okay, safe, and perfect and allowing yourself to feel good in being just that. Many of us are afraid that we are missing out, but really what we are missing out on is appreciating the moments, good and bad. We have become a society of FOMO (Fear Of Missing Out), and we sometimes take action and join in on something not because we really want to but because we are afraid we are going to miss out on something really good if we don't. This is taking action out of fear instead of inner alignment.

I'd like to look at this from another angle. Can we talk about the things you recall? Which ones really stand out in your mind? The really big ones, right? The good *and* the bad. You remember weddings, parties, vacations, illnesses, funerals, tragedies. But, do you remember the day at the beach when you found the unique shell in the sand? Or the walk in the woods when you saw the beautiful leaves? Were you fully in those moments and others like them, embodying the joy of them? Did you allow yourself to tune into your body in those moments and feel what joy, peace, and calm feel like on a physical level?

When I speak of giving yourself the gift of presence, I am talking about be-ing. Be. Be in the moments—the good, the bad, and the ugly. Each moment has something to teach us. When you are fully present in each moment, in tune and tuning in, aware, you are in the presence of you. It is a practice that takes time. I invite you to be in the discomfort. Don't label it, just feel it, experience it, imagine your breath flowing through the discomfort until it begins to shift. No need to bring it anywhere else, no need to go outside of yourself. It is an awareness of what is going on in your inner world while you are functioning in the outer world. This is my way of finding inner peace when the outside world feels uncomfortable, painful, or overwhelming.

I have had days when the outside world is chaotic, busy, loud, and overwhelming. There were times when I wished I could chill out, even though the space around me was hyped up or loud. Have you ever had this experience?

During a trip to Nashville with my close friends, I experienced a moment when I needed to stop the external noise and pause to tune inward. It was during this amazing trip that I learned I was able to be still within myself, even if the outside world was loud, overwhelming, overstimulating, or even boring. My first such experience was at a show at the Grand Ole Opry. I wanted to be at the Opry, to experience it, and it was a wonderful night and a great experience, even though I am not a country music fan. (Why the heck did I go to Nashville, right?) As we sat at the show, there were some acts that just did not hold my interest. People around me were loving them and singing along, and I decided I needed to be still and do a little self-care instead, right there in my seat. So, I closed my eyes and began to focus on my breathing, and I began to experience myself and my stillness, to learn that I can take care of my needs in the midst of chaos. I learned that the world can move around me while I stay safe within myself. I can be within myself and allow everything else to be around me but not interfere with my inner world and the experience of being calm, still, and in tune within.

I spent five to seven minutes there, within myself, and it was enough time to allow me to come back feeling energized and more interested in the show. As I watched the rest of the show, I watched myself as well, and saw that my energy and engagement with what was happening around me were more expansive. I felt amazing.

A night or two later, I found myself at another concert, this time at the Bridgestone Arena. A major headliner was going to play, and I was so excited because I love their music and had not seen them in concert for twenty years. When they arrived on the stage and started to play, I was disappointed. I was not enjoying the show and found myself wishing for it to be over quickly. Once again, I decided to go inward and focus on my breath. The energy at this concert was more intense. People were louder, the music was louder, the bass was booming. I decided to create a safe place for me even at a concert like this, and I did this by focusing on my breath and extending my energy field around my body. I imagined my heart as a huge light, surrounding my body and my energy field. When I do this, I am able to keep myself calm and safe while keeping the outside energy off of me. The space I have given myself becomes my meditation space within.

When I am in the space within, I can tap into the expansive energy around me. This energy vibrates at a higher level than the concert does. The vibrational space within allows me to tap into the creative space of self-expression. I can then hear my higher self and listen to my truth. We know when we are touching our truth, because in our truth, we are totally calm. I became calm. Instead of wanting the concert to end, I wanted to stay right where I was, experiencing inner stillness, being intimately connected to myself. Again, I learned that it is up to me to create my own safe space, my own peace, my own connection to my heart space, my own stillness and internal calm.

When we are not in our truth, we may feel fearful anxious, upset, worried, confused, off balance, disconnected, or alone. If that is the case, we must look into the feelings more deeply, almost pick them apart until we can get to the truth, to the place of calm within us. The goal is to transcend to a place of internal self-love.

It is a gift to give yourself, to be free in the moment, free of anxiety and worry. To be in the joy of it. And, even if the moment is not a good moment—because many are not—be in that too. If it is painful, be in it. Feeling uncomfortable does not mean we are going to like the feeling in the moment, but at least we are *in* the moment.

I believe the most powerful way to do this, to be present, to be on the map at the arrow that says "You Are Here" is to be one with your breath. How often are we aware of the fact that we are breathing at all? How often do we take a moment or two to stop and pay attention to our breath? People wind up having panic attacks because they haven't paid attention to their breath, and all of a sudden, they can't catch it. Do you ever stop to breathe when you are in the good moments—at the party, at the ocean? In those moments, we cannot experience anxiety, because anxiety comes from not being present. It comes from being in the future with worry or in the past with regret. Your breath is always with you, and it does not take much effort at all to remember it and pay attention to it. You don't even have to close your eyes to feel it. But, when you remember to stop and breathe, you are taking that purposeful pause. You are now empowered to be here, to focus, to feel, and to experience your breath. You are present.

What I am asking of you, as you continue to take this journey with me, is that you be in the moments of joy and fully experience them. To acknowledge your internal feelings that come with joy. To be in the moments of pain and discomfort, and fully feel them too. Do not deny your painful moments. Do not wish them away, avoid them, or stuff them down with the distractions of food, alcohol, exercise, binge watching Netflix, or getting on social media. I am asking you to be in it and feel it, and you will find that the pain will teach you what you need to learn about yourself and for yourself in that moment in order to grow.

We grow through our pain. When we avoid being present in our pain, we close off those growth opportunities. Once we allow ourselves to feel it, really allow it, it cannot be as powerful the next time it comes up. By really feeling it, we empower the self and not the pain.

You're probably wondering exactly how to go about doing this. In short, you do this by stopping the action. Imagine that you have a remote control in your hand, and at any time you can hit the pause button. As soon as you hit that button, you pause and take a breath, just like I stopped the action at the concerts. I paused and began to focus on my breathing. You become aware of both the moment and your breath.

We hear about this all of the time, about mindfulness, about being in the moment. There are all kinds of breaths you can take, and you may be familiar with several of them if you practice yoga or meditation. Many studies have proven the effectiveness of mindfulness in stress and anxiety reduction and in the ability for one's mood to lift through breathwork and meditation. I certainly cannot cover all of the research studies here, as that information is beyond the scope of this book, but be sure that I have all of this in mind as I speak to you about how invaluable a skill it is to have in your toolbox.

What I most importantly want to speak about when it comes to breathwork is the power learning to take that purposeful pause, to recognize that we need a minute. By slowing down and engaging in this pause, we transform ourselves from the guy who lives in the garbage can and flips his lid to the little red one who likes to sing and feel his feelings. We get a minute to catch our breath, gather our thoughts, listen to another, meditate for a few minutes, and give thought to the words we want to say before letting them fly out of our mouth. We get a minute to wonder, *Am I saying this from my authentic self? Or, am I saying it because I want to fix another in order to satisfy some need within me?*

If you determine that your goal is to fix another, take an even longer pause. It is never our job to fix another human being. Only they can do that. Yes, the person may need guidance, support, empathy, compassion, forgiveness, and kindness, and those things can be shared by you with them. But, if you are showing up and sharing from the energy of being here "to fix" them, do not proceed. You must first be in alignment with yourself. You must be grounded, you must feel safe—not defensive or needing to protect your own ego.

Take a breath, and be purposeful in that breath. You may even need to take a few purposeful breaths, experience what you are feeling, and ask yourself, *Whose need is being met in this moment if I open my mouth?* If it is your own need, figure out how to meet your needs without projecting them onto another. Understand that this realization indicates that the container which holds your pain has been poked.

As I hope you can see, this pause is for you. It is not for the other person. It is a moment for you to tune in and ask, *What's happening for me right now as I witness this from another?* Once you know the answer to this question, you can decide how to respond. You can then ask the other person, "What do *you* need in this moment? What will be most helpful? How can I support you in the best way for you?"

The purposeful pause is a tool that allows you to show up for yourself. It lets your heart know, "I am here for you. I did not forget you. I care about you. You matter. I see you." The magic happens because we are slowing down and tuning in, which we so often forget to do. We may notice a feeling that our heart is racing, but do not slow down for even a moment to help our own heart out of its racing pace. I beg the question, why not? Why don't we slow down enough for our self? Imagine how you are able to create a powerful shift in your life just by slowing down for a moment and tuning in to you and remembering that the arrow is pointing to indicate "You Are Here."

Imagine, if you slowed down enough to pause, take a breath and tune in—even for only two minutes—how much more you could accomplish. By slowing down and taking that breath, you are breaking a pattern of ignoring you, of always being on the run, of your mind jumping from one idea to the next. You actually create space. This space that you are creating is the space where healing begins. No one on the outside can create this space for you, nothing on the outside can create this space for you. It is yours and yours alone, and therefore, only you can create it.

We are told to go outside into nature and connect with the beach, the woods, the mountain trail. It is lovely to be in those beautiful outdoor spaces, but if your mind is stuck in a story of something else, you are really not there, are you? You are not present. I agree with the value of going to a place that brings you joy. When you bring your physical body to a location that you find peaceful, quiet, invigorating, or inspiring, be sure to bring your mind along too. That means that when you get there, you take a purposeful pause in order to focus on your breath, be present, feel your feet on the ground, touch a leaf, feel the sand, smell a flower, hug a tree, lift your face to the sun or the moon, feel the air, dance in the rain, or otherwise be present and reconnect to yourself.

You do not have to go anywhere to do this. As I write this chapter, I am sitting at my desk. I stopped and took a purposeful pause because I noticed my heart was racing. I did not know why. So, I stopped. I took a few breaths with my feet on the floor, sending love to my racing heart until it calmed down. As soon as I connected with myself, I came back into balance, addressed the reason for the racing, and was able to get back to writing. I am always in awe of the universe. Every time I need to be shown something, to understand it more deeply, to be more aware, I am given a way. My way in this moment, on this particular morning, was to take the pause.

When you pause, you get to be connected to yourself. Once you connect to the true essence of who you are, you find your inner compass and peaceful place. All of us want to find the peace that lies within us. In fact, at some level of your being, you have always known it was there. The way to peace is a path that begins and ends within us. But how does one get on the path, and what will we find along the way? How can we hold onto the path of peace if suddenly we find ourselves in the middle of a storm--a storm we are not prepared for, a storm we did not see coming? Do we take cover? Do we put up a blockade? Do we storm back, attempting to become bigger and scarier, thinking we can fight the storm...and win? Or, do we put on our rain gear and enter the storm, becoming one with the wind and the rain, welcoming it and deciding to ride it out because, right now, we are in it, and no action can change it beyond it coming to its own logical and natural end.

These are also times when taking a pause is critical. As you ride out the storm, you can find peace and calm within your own being and know—really know—that even though you are in this big storm, you are safe. You have not gotten blown off your path. The path is right there beneath your feet the whole time. You are stable, you are secure, you are present. And you learn over and over again that you can trust yourself, trust your path, and stay ever peaceful. Taking the purposeful pause will help you ride out the storms of life more easily. Yes, the storms will still come, life happens, but the pause is a great tool that I offer to you to allow you to flow with it more easily.

Any time you become anxious, here is an exercise that will help bring you into the present moment and reclaim a calm state. Remember, it is when you are in the present moment that you are acutely aware that there is no anxiety.

Journal Prompts

- Take a moment right now to take a few breaths and pause with purpose.

- Pay close attention to your surroundings and begin to talk to yourself. What time of day is it? Where are you? Are you sitting on the couch, chair, floor? For example, say to yourself, "It is Monday at 9am. I am home; it is sunny out. I am on the blue couch, the walls are white, my pants are blue, and I am eating breakfast." Keep doing this to reorient yourself until you feel yourself becoming calmer.

- Feel your breaths, experience them, and as you do, tune into yourself. Ask yourself some more questions. How does my body feel right now? Is it comfortable or uncomfortable? If it is comfortable, pay attention to what it feels like to experience comfort. If it is uncomfortable, pay attention to the pain and the chakra where you are experiencing that discomfort.

- Take a breath and one to two minutes and allow the feeling of pain the pass through you.

- Be in the awareness of the pain, and remember, it only lasts for that moment. It will then move, and you will move into the next moment where the pain can be different—perhaps less intense.

- See what shows up for you in your body.

CHAPTER 10

The Spiral of Healing

In 2015 I was away at a retreat. This particular retreat center, in the mountains of upstate New York, had a meditation room. It was an odd room off the rear of the house; you had to climb up a short staircase to enter it. The ceiling of the staircase was low, so you had to climb while ducking your head at the same time. When I entered this room for the first time, I felt as if I was in a very sacred and special place. To the naked eye, it looked like any other meditation room or yoga room, but I deeply felt this room. I was drawn there each morning to do my own silent meditation. During these meditations, I listened to the lessons I was being given, which were the messages for this book. I knew it at the time that I would be writing this book, but I did not know how or when the opportunity would present itself.

As I sat in that meditation room the very first morning, I lit a candle at the altar and set my intention, which was to be open to receiving whatever I needed to know for my highest and greatest good. The inner knowing I received that very first morning was the following:

You are open and ready to receive all that is, do not let ego get in the way. Whatever the words are that come into your mind are desired for today. Do not judge, do not edit, do not be afraid. As you walk this journey, you are not alone. There are many warriors who stand by your side, victims, both seen and unseen. As you light your light, you are helping and healing those who are also suffering. Especially those who are suffering in silence. You cannot know the impact your light has, as it is not for you to know, because that is ego. It must be enough to just know. In the knowing, you will find your greatest strength. In the trusting, you will find the greatest knowing. Be not afraid of the dark. The dark has much to teach as well. When you can be in the dark and be your light, your greatest light, then you find that you are your own greatest truth seeker. No one else can teach you this.

Reading this back, I was blown away. How was it that *I* was able to experience this kind of inner knowing? I began to wonder, *Is it really up to me to share with the world what I am learning? Who am I to know this? Who am I to teach this? I am just a girl from Brooklyn who has been on her own journey to heal.* Needless to say, I was overwhelmed.

After this experience, I knew I would be back each morning for the rest of the weekend. I could not wait for all of it to unfold. The quality of the insights and wisdom I was receiving this particular weekend were new to me. I was open and ready. And those two components are key ingredients in doing this work. We must be open and ready to accept whatever it is that is showing up for us in the present. We cannot sit in judgement or second guess it (though I admit that sometimes, it's hard not to). I often sit in awe of the process, knowing that the insights that come to us during meditation could never be made up. Even in our imagination, we would not come up with the words and images that come through. In very basic terms, "You can't make this stuff up."

On day two, I this was the inner knowing I received:

You have been giving love and healing from your heart, and in doing this you are raising your own vibration even higher. Allow yourself to continue to be drawn to the others who are in need of healing, because as you step into the energy of their healing, you also receive. The place you went to with Andrew last night is actually available to all who desire to go. The method of arriving is with an open, uninhibited heart. This is a place for cellular renewal and healing as was experienced last night by those present. Each one present received a healing which raised the vibrational frequency they work with. Andrew was like a conduit, connecting through him many points of light which allowed his cells, in a sense, to be reborn. There was great growth for him in emotional places that still needed some TLC. There is a new freedom to love in a greater and more fulfilling way. To experience a shared love which is like the

144 • JANET PHILBIN

infinity symbol flowing between two hearts. Your gifts as a healer continue to grow. There is confusion now, and you are searching to others to give you clarification or validation as to the next step on your path. These decisions will not come from others, but will come from what you hear from yourself. Continue to trust yourself in all ways. You did make a shift at the labyrinth yesterday. You released a layer and replaced it with light. You know your work. You know your path. Keep trusting faith, love, patience of self and others. These are gifts. Love, patience, kindness; gifts of the open heart.

I was suddenly aware of what was happening. The previous evening, I'd led a group healing session for Andrew. It was a very powerful experience for all of us, and we needed to understand what that experience was.

Our insights are there to give us guidance. The way to access the healing ability in each of us is to arrive with an open and uninhibited heart. When we can arrive at the doorstep of our own healing process with an open heart, without judgement, without resistance, and with trust, we can fully step into the experience, receive what is being offered to us, and receive all of the necessary lessons for healing. I did not know exactly what lesson I was going to learn, but I knew I was being prepared for something big.

I was becoming clear that, beyond all else, I must trust myself. This is a key component; you must trust yourself. You must trust in your inner knowing. You must look beyond your anxieties and fears and judgements and listen to your heart. Your heart will lead the way if you allow it to do so. Maybe your heart will lead you to the right therapist, healer, yoga teacher, class, or book. Follow it. You will not be led astray. Did your heart lead you to this book? How did you end up picking up this particular book to read? How are the words in this book speaking to your heart?

Pause here to listen to the answers that your heart has for you. The answers lie within you. This book will not give you the answers but will instead lead you to the places inside of your heart that have been longing for understanding and waiting to be heard. Within your heart lies your light, that light you were born with that we spoke about earlier. It is still there within you. You get to touch it again, feel it again, and support yourself to brighten your light and turn up the dimmer switch so that it can shine at full power.

When I arrived at the altar on Sunday morning, the inner knowing and wisdom I received about healing was:

Thank you for coming and being ready to listen. You must trust first that you will allow the vibration to come through you to shed all fear, to shed all doubt, to step aside of ego, and to be one with the one and know that this is who you already are and who you have always been. You are a star being of the brightest light. There was a choice to come to human form to experience the full expanse of human emotion. To understand the depths of pain and rejoice in the joy to know what it means to heal. To know what it means to feel shame. To know what it means to feel guilt and emotional conflict. These feelings that those in human form wish to avoid are actually the greatest gifts. These are the places where the most learning is done. There are no accidents in the light. You are given what is needed at the time, and ego is the most open and ready for your growth. Without first going to the depths of pain, there would be no cry for help. When the ego releases, it is no longer in control. It releases and you can hear the answers given in the cry for help. This is the way of the light. Your heart holds the flame of the wisdom of the light. When you are in the light of your heart, you are intuitive, you are a healer. You have always been a healer, and this runs in the cell structure of the human form you take. It has been experienced in many ways, even as a child. It is in the cells that are carried in your soul and these soul cells are brought to each incarnation to experience the learning you come in seeking. You are a seeker.

Needless to say, I was in awe of what I was realizing—that I *needed* the pain, conflict, shame, and guilt. That these big feelings, feelings that I—and most of us—want to avoid, were actually gifts. My left brain could not wrap itself around this idea for quite some time. I wanted to heal, and I knew that it was my journey to heal. But to come to understand that my pain was a gift to me? That was an idea I deeply wanted to resist. Maybe you do too. But somewhere deep inside, I knew it was a truth I would need to come to accept and understand or else there would be no growth.

The path to understanding this more deeply lay in the insight I needed to understand more clearly, which was that when the ego releases, it is no longer in control, and you can hear the answers given to your cry for help. I did not get it then. I did not know the ego as I know it now. Back then, in 2015, when I thought of ego, I thought of Freud. Remember, I am traditionally trained in Western psychology, and at that point I had only a bit of knowledge of the Eastern philosophy I have now come to embrace. I knew the ego as bravado, as pride, as an overinflated sense of self. But that is no longer what I know ego to be.

The ego is the false self. As it is understood in Eastern philosophy, the ego came to be as a way to protect the inner child. When we needed to survive in childhood whatever we were experiencing, a part of us needed to hide, and we developed a false self to protect the true essence of who we are. So, the ego grew in order to protect us. It grew to keep us safe. But really, this ego must be kept in check with a close and careful eye. It needs to release the belief that it has to stay in control. When it does, when we are able to shed the ego, our true essence can be in the lead, and we can *be* our light. At that point, we can heal at a cellular level.

The healing process that I call The Spiral of Healing is what I learned next. I would not have been able to understand the lesson about the Spiral of Healing if I did not first understand the lessons that came before. It is important to understand that there are no shortcuts to healing.

There is nothing on the outside that will fix our emotional holes. All the work to become emotionally *whole* must be done from the inside. Healing on the spiral is an inside-out process. I have always known that; in fact, it is my philosophy in my counseling practice. This new layer of understanding simply gave me a framework to comprehend it more clearly.

Before I share the Spiral of Healing more thoroughly, I want to offer you an insight from the book *Walking on the wind* by Michael T. Garrett. This book teaches of the Cherokee beliefs and principles about harmony and balance. In the Cherokee belief system, it is said that all things have spiritual energy and importance. I know this to be true based on my own life experiences. The Cherokee believe in the necessity of harmony and balance by emphasizing the following: everything is a circle, everything has a purpose, all things are connected, and we can embrace the medicine of all living things as we work together in the circle. Medicine, as defined by the Cherokee is "something that every living being possesses. It is an inner power or way of life which connects us to all living beings through our hearts. A person's medicine is their power, their energy, their essence."

In the Cherokee tradition, the circle reflects the relationship of all living beings and the natural progression of life itself. It is a sacred symbol that serves as a reminder of the circular nature of all of life's energy. As you travel up the Spiral in Healing, you also travel in a circular motion. The Cherokee teach that all things are important in the

circle, and we are to remember the sacred interrelation-
ship of all and the clarity that comes when you open yourself up to the energy of the circle of life. The same is true
for the Spiral of Healing. As you heal up the spiral, understand that this is sacred work you are embarking on. It is
the sacred work of healing yourself at a cellular level, of
healing on a level of the seen (form) and unseen (formless).

The Spiral of Healing is a circle that rises. It is within
this circle that we touch upon our own medicine, our life
force energy, and come to know our hearts and the fact
that we do not walk this journey alone but in connection
to others, the Earth, and spirit.

Here is what I knew to be true after that weekend retreat:

*In order to find, you must feel-heal-grow-love. That is the
cycle: feel-heal-grow-love. Each time you complete a cycle,
you raise your vibration and open your gifts, not just your
intuitive gifts but all of your gifts in humanity to heal the
self. To heal the self with understanding, love, and forgiveness, as you have been taught by your teachers. They
teach as they continue their own journey of feel-heal-
grow-love. Do not be afraid of the journey. It is the journey
of light that is being given at this time to aid in understanding of self and healing in relationship with others.
There cannot be doubt in the love and light of God. This is
forgotten at times. Many insights have been shared this
weekend, journeys to places that no one expected, journey*

to the depths of souls and to the highest of light. This has been shown and shared with all to learn that there can be no doubt when you are in God's love. Be free, be in God's love. Trust self.

There it was. I was speechless, and trust me, I am rarely speechless. Luckily, I still had the last day of the retreat weekend to sit with it before I had to reenter my life at home. In order to help myself understand it better, I decided to draw it out.

This is how I first saw the Spiral of Healing and drew it in my journal that morning. I want you to understand the circular nature of the process; there really is no beginning and no end. There is no particular order. As you can see, the arrows go around and around, each touching the next, only to come back around again.

The Spiral of Healing is like a helix, and all aspects of the self are on this helix. I like to think of the spiral as our emotional DNA. This DNA can be reprogrammed and healed through meditation, hypnosis, energy healing, and other healing modalities. As you move up and around the spiral, you heal aspects of the wounded self. The new, healed aspect takes the place of the aspect that was previously hurting. This is why it is a spiral that goes upwards instead of being flat. As we heal, we rise.

It starts deep inside our inner child. It starts at the very beginning within us, from the very first time that our inner child had to hide to feel protected. It is a continuous process of feel-heal-grow-love. Every time you leave one level and go to the next, you touch the old as you grow into the next. We go around, we retouch, we grow. We can't erase the memories, but as we are on the spiral we are always moving upward. When we are again triggered, that new trigger represents another aspect of something we touched on a lower level of the spiral but are now looking at and feeling from a different vantage point because we have grown. We can perhaps also handle being able to look at or feel the pain more deeply and gain a new understanding about our self and our process.

The spiral is a place for you to go, explore, and then assess how you are doing. It is not a cookie cutter approach or a step-by-step guide. When you are in your process of healing on the spiral, you can begin to ask yourself questions as self-assessments. These questions include:

- *Where am I?*
- *What am I doing?*
- *Am I allowing myself to feel my feelings?*
- *Is this a space where growth is happening?*
- *Is healing happening in the growth?*
- *Do I have to heal something else here before I can move onto something else and grow?*

It's important that you take time to process and understand each level of the spiral. Even though I will explain each aspect separately in the next chapters, understand that they happen simultaneously as you go around and up the Spiral of Healing. Each layer is to be explored before going to the next. It is about understanding yourself at the current level of your heart and understanding how each level affects your heart's growth and opening. The full and open loving heart is a gift to be treasured. Being in a place full of an open, loving heart allows for transformation. It allows one to shed anxiety and fear. Even shadow is no match for the full and open loving heart.

Each level is a lesson. Each lesson holds layers of understanding through which you will move. This method of feel-heal-grow-love is one through which you can release fear. It is a method for healing.

"What we hold onto holds us back."

Holding onto anything is like emotional bondage that we keep our self-trapped within. If you have trapped yourself, it is within your power to release the bond that holds so you can find your way to emotional freedom. All that you need is to find a way to undo the points of bondage that lie within you. We are afraid to look inside because we fear what we may find. We may have to look at our fears, stories, pain, limiting beliefs, projections, and self-sabotage. It's a process that requires brutal honesty. There may be layers to go through and stories to reexamine in

154 • JANET PHILBIN

order to find the truth.

The Spiral of Healing is always there waiting for you. The journey is not somewhere over there or at some other time in your life. It's with you in this very moment. It's part of you and everything that you are.

Approaching the journey may feel a lot like approaching a roller coaster. You may feel paralyzed by fear, your feet might not move, you might hate the feeling of being out of control, you might hate the feeling of your stomach dropping as the ride takes a plunge. You are afraid to scream because you worry whether someone will hear you, or even worse, that perhaps no one will. You might feel alone, unsupported, and in uncharted territory.

What is the story you have told yourself about yourself when it comes to winding up in this space? *If I go forward, I will die, be ashamed, crumble to the ground.* For me, all those years ago, when I even thought about facing everything I needed to heal through, everything I needed to face in order to heal, I was afraid I would begin screaming and never stop. The reality was, that did not happen. I have become stronger than I ever could have anticipated. Have you stood there before, ready to face that ride, and then turned away, only to find you had walked in a circle and were still lost, left to face the same fear of healing you continued to turn away from?

I know that feeling. It took me a long time and a lot of therapy to get through it. My Spiral of Healing was terrifying, and I therefore built a huge brick wall in front of me. My belief system at the time was, "No way, no how, is it coming down." I would stay safe above all else with my feet on the ground. The one problem with keeping that wall up was that, with it up, I was unable to grow. You cannot block one aspect of yourself from growing and blooming and expect others to grow and bloom. As Brene Brown says, you cannot numb only one feeling or part of you. When you numb one part, you numb them all. We are always faced with the choice when it comes to whether or not to get on the ride that healing will take us on—the choice to grow, the choice toward self-love. Ride it up, see what you encounter, welcome it, and as you do, even with the pain—and actually, *because* of the pain—you can heal.

Over the months that followed the retreat, I continued to meditate on this concept. I wanted to more deeply understand the Spiral of Healing and how it is intended to work. What follows is the insight and wisdom about the Spiral of Healing I have continued to gain:

To be in the love of all that is eternal, the knowing that comes from within a soul that cries out, "It is time to be heard." Do not turn your back on the growth that is within you. You have seen the weeds. Don't get stuck in the weeds. The weeds have shallow roots and try their hardest to look pretty, all while being destructive to the flowers that have deep roots. We cannot get stuck in the weeds of the mind because we will get trapped, suffocated, and cut off. The weeds represent surface emotions, not the deeper feelings. The weeds fool us, because we recognize them and they look pretty to us in their form. It is time to pull them out of the soil and till the soil; the soil is now ready for renewal, for growth, for TLC.

Are you brave enough to go forward and do this work? You have asked for help. You have been heard and are now being answered by the seeds you have hidden in your heart. You are now ready to plant them. These are the parts that need healing, the parts that have been deeply asking to see and feel the light because they have been in pain and are tired of carrying the burden.

The roots grow from the seeds, and the roots tap into the healing vibrations. They grow so that you can heal. Healing is a process of growth. Just like the root must burst through the shell of the seed, we too must burst through the shell of the seed. We must burst through the pain of our shell to begin to put the healing roots of our lost selves into the Earth. To begin to absorb the rich nutrients of the soil, to drink up the water, all of this allows for growth.

Just recently in meditation, I once again desired insights on the Spiral of Healing, as I was seeking more clarification. What I came to understand is that each time we start on a new level of the spiral, we do so from a new level of learning, but our consciousness may say, "I have learned this lesson before." However, we have not heard it with the same level of evolvement, therefore we take it into our cells differently the next time around. We allow it to penetrate the depths of our being as we become the master of that which sits in front of us. When we master it at that level, we are ready to move on to the next level in order to process it through *that* lens, those filters, those cells until we reach the next level of becoming. It is all part of growth and evolution. Some only get so far; they feel content staying where they are. Some will get stuck on a spot in the spiral before they are ready to move again. Some will slide backward. Others will always crave more. This is the journey the planet is on right now, and there are many seekers of this knowledge and truth.

The greatest gifts are there within you to help you uncover the sovereign truth of your soul. As you travel the spiral, you will embark on the journey to the center of yourself, where you find the true calling of your heart. It is in the heart space that you can hear the beloved messages of truth that are there for you each and every day.

The healing you seek is the love that you are.

The love that you seek is the connection of your soul to source energy; to oneness; to wholeness; to inner peace, wisdom, tranquility, and love. Do not be afraid to venture forward and make these connections. You do not need others to reach your goals. You only need a roadmap or blueprint to get *you* started. This Spiral of Healing is that starting point, that roadmap.

Growing and healing on the spiral is a process to help you understand that growth is a process of breaking free from the trappings of your ego. Once you can break free, the ability to heal and grow is vast and full of limitless po-

158 • JANET PHILBIN

tential. It is up to you to ask yourself, "What do I need to break free from?" "What has kept me encaged?" "What have I been so afraid of that I have made a choice to stay stuck?" No one can answer these questions for you. These answers must come from you. Take a breath, close your eyes, ask yourself those questions, and write down the answers below. Allow yourself to be *in* the feelings, experience the feelings, and identify the feelings.

Journal prompts

- What do I need to break free from?

- What has kept me caged?

- What have I been so afraid of that I have made the choice to stay stuck?

- Where in my body do I feel and experience these feelings?

- Which chakra is affected?

- How does the feeling look? (describe with details)

- What, in my imagination, do those feelings need in order to heal?

The next chapter explores each of the components of the Spiral of Healing. At times, you will see that part of a particular section actually seems like it should be in another. The reason for this is that all of these moving pieces do not happen in linear fashion. In fact, the process of feel, heal, grow, love is one that happens at times separately, and at times simultaneously. I have deconstructed it into a separate chapter to help you digest and understand each part individually.

CHAPTER 11

Feel, Heal, Grow, Love

FEEL

Feel: *verb*: to be aware of, something that affects you physically, such as pain, heat, or an object touching your body. To be conscious of an inward impression, state of mind, or physical condition. To touch (something) with your fingers to see what it is like. To find (something) by touching with your fingers. To be aware of by instinct or inference. To perceive by a physical sensation coming from discrete end organs (as of the skin or muscles).

—Merriam-Webster dictionary

Let's begin by taking a look at the "feel" component of the Spiral of Healing. Feel, as you will discern from the Merriam-Webster dictionary definition, is a verb, an action. It means that something is happening. We are either taking action to physically touch someone or something, or we have an awareness of something that is physically affecting us, either internally or externally.

My own definition of the word feel is "to allow yourself to experience a sensation within you." To feel is to touch and experience the texture of the sensation, to consciously experience what happens on the inside.

When you have a feeling in your body, it can, at times, be very subtle. The unconscious mind, however, picks up on them, at which point the feeling then becomes a thought. A feeling comes up in the body, but in a split second, we tell a story to ourselves about the feeling, which brings us out of the body and into the mind. Once that feeling enters the mind as a thought, we no longer feel it or let it pass through. We get stuck in "thinking about the thought." It takes only sixty to ninety seconds for a feeling to pass through the body. This transition from feeling to thought in the thinking mind happens in seconds. In fact, it happens so fast that we are not even consciously aware of the transition from feeling to thought. Instead of allowing for that moment to experience the sensation and allow the feeling to pass, we develop a story around the feeling. Because the feeling may be subtle, the conscious mind is not aware that the feeling actually began in the body and it's not a story at all.

Many people walk around in a state of total disconnect from their physical experiences as feelings. They interpret the physical sensation of a feeling as "not feeling well" when, in reality, it is just "butterflies in your stomach," which is a sensation, or "feeling" one is experiencing. Feelings start in the physical body, and we are always aware of the big ones. Emotions are our minds' reactions to feelings. The emotion is the label we give to the experience of the physical feelings.

The Merriam-Webster dictionary definition of emotion is "a conscious mental reaction (such as anger or fear) subjectively experienced as strong feeling usually directed toward a specific object and typically accompanied by physiological and behavioral changes in the body." Even from this definition, it is easy to understand that emotions are labels we assign to a feeling, either behavioral or physiological, that begins in the body.

For example, we experience a sensation in our stomach that can be described as fluttering. However, perhaps every time you experience this fluttering, you associate it with nervousness, and now, all of a sudden, you declare that you are nervous. You may even describe yourself as "a nervous wreck," indicating that you are identifying with the feeling even more strongly. Calling yourself a nervous wreck then becomes an identity you refer to in order to define part of who you are instead of just allowing the feeling of fluttering in your stomach to be simply that: a feeling of fluttering.

A feeling of fluttering is not who you are, it is an experience you are having.

When you can be conscious and make a distinction between the person you are and the feeling you are experiencing, you are not attaching your identity to the feeling. This offers you freedom. When we label a feeling, we give it all sorts of attributes and meanings. Our emotions then become thoughts related to the way we are making sense of our experiences, both internally and externally. Those thoughts can then turn into a story that we get stuck in. The story is almost always about the past or future that we are projecting our current state onto, which brings us right out of the present moment of feeling something. When we are able to connect the dots between them—the feeling, emotion and thought, and finally the insight, growth and healing can begin.

The next time a particular feeling comes up and you do not pay attention to it from a state of consciousness, you will go right into the replay of the story you previously developed. You will then attach blame, anger, guilt, or frustration to the story. It is easy, at that point, to externalize and project your feelings out of the self, enabling the original feeling to get stuck in the body and wreak emotional and physical havoc. The end result may be that we become depressed, anxious, or physically ill in the area where the chakra has gotten stuck. We end up stuck in time in our mind at the event, feeling, or story. We are not present; we are reacting from an unconscious place.

We are always works in progress. I am always in awe when I have an experience that brings me back to a core issue. I now know, however, that it is because I am riding this spiral upward, and as part of that ride, I now need to look at this core issue again—but from a different point of view. I want to share with you two examples of how this has happened for me and how I was able to move through these challenges. Challenges show up for us to teach us something about our self—for us, for our growth, and for our emotional evolution.

In the first example, I was taking an online class for which we had to use a workbook to process the exercises. What follows is an excerpt from that exercise, in which I was to look back at a recent time when I was triggered. I referenced a situation that happened with one of my children during which I felt I was being yelled at. Here is what I wrote in my workbook:

I was triggered because I hate being yelled at, because I do not feel I deserve it. I felt I did not deserve to be yelled at because I was with my child all day, and I had been caring, patient, compassionate and felt my child was just being emotional at me. I was triggered because I feel I can never do enough or anything right. I was afraid. I am afraid I am not a good enough mom.

Holy SH*T! There is was, in black and white, right in front of me. Honestly, I was shocked. That feeling of not being good enough was still there, showing up after all the inner healing work I have done, after all the conscious parenting I have practiced. I knew I was reactive, but my child was coming at me with such energy, and after thirty minutes, I could not contain it anymore and yelled back. I was trapped in the car, driving. There was nowhere to go. And, without a means to physically leave and get space, I went back to an old reaction, which was to yell.

In the moment when something is happening, those old feelings still show up, get our attention, and bring us back to the feelings. The feeling I had in my body was tension, and let me tell you, that tension was diffused, touching all of my chakras. The thing to remember, and the reason I used this example, is that the trigger is never on the outside, it is *always* on the inside. When I was experiencing the feeling of being yelled at, helpless and stuck, it poked an old wound. It is our internal wound, one that is rooted in fear, that is getting poked. That is exactly what happened to me. I knew it in the moment and immediately began breathing and bringing myself back from that proverbial edge and into my conscious awareness. In doing this, I was able to stop yelling and find some degree of balance.

Another example of this process showing up for me occurred even more recently. My mother died in March of 2019. A few months later, I was driving home from work, and for whatever reason, I began to think about her. A feeling came over me in that moment, and it was a feeling of deep missing. In that moment, I felt empty. I was able to tune in to my awareness and know what I needed to do in that moment when that empty feeling, that feeling of missing her, came over me. I had to just let myself feel it, experience it, and then allow it to pass through me. The way to allow this is in the moment of the big feelings is to focus on your breath. That is what I did as I drove. I focused on my breath and the way my breath felt as it entered and left my body while I experienced the powerful feeling that was hurting my heart chakra. Remember, it only takes sixty to ninety seconds for a feeling to rise up and then pass through us. I knew in that moment that if I could allow myself to feel it, to be fully in the experience of missing her, it would quickly pass and I would be able to move on. Doing this gave me space so that I did not have to get attached to a story. The story could have been "Now I am a motherless daughter. What does that mean for me in my life?" I could have had a huge pity party all by myself. Once the feelings passed through me, I was able to sit with myself and my feelings in the present moment, accepting that in that moment, that was the feeling that came up. I needed to accept that it was allowed to come up, and that I was okay.

I want to take some time to dig into what it means to feel your feelings. To feel, we must experience it all. We must go to the depths of the pain, explore it, and allow ourselves to touch it, just as I did in the above example.

Let me explain it another way. Have you ever jumped into the deep end of a pool? Once you jumped in, did you ever try to stop yourself halfway down because you didn't want to touch the bottom of the deep end? It is quite difficult to stop yourself when you're already halfway down. It takes a lot more work and uses a great deal of both mental and physical energy. Does one even stop to wonder why she doesn't want to go with the flow of it, quite literally, and just touch the bottom? If you do not touch the bottom, you have to find a way to stop the downward motion and get back up to the surface. Once you break the surface, you are treading water, stuck in the deep end, not able to see the side of the pool. Feeling fatigued and like you are drowning, you call for help (or maybe you don't), but without having anything to touch or grab you'll flounder because you do not yet know that you have the ability to save yourself. However, when you let yourself reach the bottom, you get to push yourself back up to break the surface where you can breathe again. Once you touch, you can swim to the side and save yourself. Saving yourself is empowering, it is validation to you, from you, that yes, you have the power to do this work and heal.

Feeling the sensations and pain is like touching the bottom of the deep end of the pool. Once you do, you can push off, come to the surface, and breathe again. But so many of us are afraid to touch and experience those feelings. Instead, we avoid them and expend a lot of physical and mental energy in that avoidance; it is exhausting.

Let me return to what it means to feel. To feel means to be *in* the experience, to be *in* the truth of the moment as it is happening, when it is happening. Not to fight the truth but to recognize it. In that recognition comes a knowing, and this knowing is called a feeling. The feeling may be wide and all-encompassing, or it may be small and manageable. But it's a feeling experience nonetheless, and one not to ignore. Ignored feelings simmer like water in a pot, and if untended the pot gets burned once the water evaporates. The burn leaves a mark, a scar, an imprint, which then needs to be repaired. This is what happens to unattended feelings over time.

However, if we carefully pay attention to the simmering pot, that pot won't get burned before we take it off the stove. Taking the pot off of the stove is like paying attention to the feeling. Once paid attention to, the feeling can begin to calm down, just as we can begin to calm down, because we're at a point where we are no longer ignoring the self.

What good does it do to ignore the self? What does it lead to? It may lead to a sense of not being valued, a belief of worthlessness, or a story that says, "I am not important." All of those thoughts are ego, the false self, and the experience of those thoughts may feel bad. You may cry, get a stomachache, feel a tightness in your chest or throat. Do you pay attention to the feelings that are under the thoughts, or do you stay stuck in the thought? Staying stuck in the thought and the subsequent thoughts and stories indicates that you're not paying attention to feelings.

Instead, tell yourself that you are valued and important, and that you matter. You, above all others, know who you are. Do not be swayed by others. Everything is tied together; nothing happens in a bubble. We must have an intimate knowledge of how something feels, and journaling helps us get to this knowing by allowing us to look at and explore the experience of what we are feeling.

Before we move on to heal, I want to briefly talk about reacting and reenacting, because both come from an unconscious place connected to our feelings. To react means to respond or behave in a particular way in response to something. It also means to respond with hostility, opposition, or a contrary course of action. Reactivity is a form of self-protection, like a porcupine's quills coming out. When you go into reactivity, you are really protecting the self, the ego. The ego does not want the true self to emerge, because the ego is afraid that if the true self speaks, the ego will be rejected.

To reenact, on the other hand, means to act out a past event. To take it one step further, when you react you are actually reenacting. You are reenacting old behaviors based on old feelings from an old story. This happens because our unconscious mind has no sense of time. So, when a feeling comes up in the present moment, and it's similar to an unhealed feeling from the past, you are still operating from your wounded inner child and working really hard to resolve the unresolved feelings that were originally ignored. The problem is, you are not going to be successful at resolving them by using old coping skills and relying on the old story to validate your present feelings. Using the old story as a valid reason in the present is like trying to force together two mismatched puzzle pieces, and I know from my many experiences with jigsaw puzzles that this approach does not work.

Let's recall that feelings are called feelings because they are felt. We feel them first, and the place where we feel them is the physical body. When you feel a feeling in the physical body, it is up to you to take notice of it and give it those sixty to ninety seconds to be felt and to pass through you. When you halt the feelings in their tracks, they get stuck in the body, at which point you give the feeling a name like fear, worry, upset, or stress, and then the story starts. That's how feelings get stuck—you don't allow them to flow through you. Then, when the feeling comes up again, you react to it by reenacting old patterns and behaviors.

In the future, when this feeling now stuck in your body gets "triggered," you instantly pull up the story from your unconscious and begin to reenact it. The inner child reenacts the emotions of the untended-to feelings. The inner child, in the form of the adult self, reenacts this pain that initially went untended.

Sometimes, we act out against the self through addictions. Addictions to food, sex, love, screens, substances like drugs or alcohol, or maybe exercise, strict regimental routines, or perfectionism. Regardless, we act them out through reenactment, and that reenactment hurts not only us but the people closest to us. I am not an addiction specialist. To really explore and understand addiction, I invite you to find the experts in the area of addiction that is affecting you or your loved ones. For the purposes of this book, I am briefly touching on the subject because we often turn to addiction to fill a part of us that feels empty or in pain. In other words, we are looking outside of ourselves to fill holes in order to feel whole. This will not work. It's neither healing nor healthy.

I was at a conference in the spring of 2019 with Dr. Steven Dewey, Ph.D., a research professor at New York University who has been researching the effects of addictive drugs on the human brain. At the conference, he explained addiction as a complex neurochemical disease, much the same way depression, bipolar disease, and ADHD are complex diseases. We cannot talk about addiction without understanding dopamine. Dopamine is a neurotransmitter that changes the most in addiction. Dopamine's primary role is movement. It allows one to feel pleasure. The natural reward we get when we feel pleasure is an increase in our dopamine levels by four to five percent. If we experience something sad or unpleasant, our dopamine levels *decrease* by four to five percent.

In essence, and for the sake of simplicity, we can increase our dopamine naturally. If you go running, you get the four to five percent increase in dopamine and feel the runner's high. However, if someone is using drugs, dopamine levels are raised millions of times. What happens in addiction, no matter what one is addicted to, is that one is always chasing the dopamine high. Whenever you use something outside of you to fill a hole within you, you become addicted to the outside source and begin to rely on this outside source instead of yourself. The outside source can be the person you are in a relationship with, your parent, your child, your job, your mobile device, or a substance.

In today's society, one of the most common addictions is to our phones and social media. We have become programmed to look at these devices and platforms. We don't want to miss out on anything. We need to know if someone liked, commented, or shared our post. We want to know how many followers we have. Each time the phone "dings," we experience the high of a dopamine hit. Has your phone ever beeped, and you were able to resist picking it up? If so, did you notice that you had anxiety about not grabbing it to see who was pinging you? If so, that's an indicator of being addicted.

Dr. Dewey also conducted a study that proved that obesity meets all of the criteria for addiction. Imagine that: obesity meets addiction criteria. In order to become obese, you need to consume a lot of food. Food is also used to fill those holes inside of us. Once again, the person who uses food to self-soothe is looking outside to feel better on the inside. Dr. Dewey also studied Mobile Phone Dependence (MPD). He concluded through the use of PET scans that dopamine levels in the brain increased by sixty-five percent when teenagers held *their* phone versus a smartphone of an alternate brand. And, guess what? The brain lit up more when they held their phone versus someone else's. We are even addicted to the *feel* of the phone.

Why am I telling you all of this? Because we are turning away from ourselves, we are not relying on our own inner resources to help us heal the holes inside of us. Instead, we are looking out. Looking out to fix what is broken on the inside by looking outside of the self. It is like chasing a cloud; you can never catch it. It will always be out of reach. The only way to fill those holes and heal them so you can be whole again is to do the work from the inside out. You must go inside, get to the bottom of the pain, and engage on the Spiral of Healing through all of its levels. Then and only then will the desire and need to look outside for validation, soothing, and the removal of pain be able to be taken care of by and for you. You can use healthy methods of self-care like eating good food, exercising, meditating, journaling, being in nature, and more because these things are good for you.

It is up to you to bring the unconscious into the conscious. To be aware, mindful, and present everyday as much as possible. To look at what is getting acted out. To sit and look within to discover where the feelings are coming from and ask some questions.

Can you identify these feelings in your day-to-day life? If so, which ones? Which get acted out with your partner, children, family, or friends? How are they acted out? When you act them out, what need are you really asking to be met? And, when you act out, are those needs truly met?

It is up to you to feel the feeling instead of giving it a label, which only becomes an emotion you identify yourself with and then act out. When you catch yourself *before* you get stuck in the story, you are allowing yourself to be in the feelings and on the Spiral of Healing.

Journal Prompts

- Think about the most recent time you were triggered. Pause and tune into your body.

- What is the physical sensation you are experiencing? Describe it.

- What thoughts and stories have been attached to this feeling?

- What do you really need in this moment for self-care?

HEAL

Heal: *verb*: To become healthy or well again. To make
sound or whole <*heal* a wound>. 2. To patch up (a breach
or division) 3. To restore to original purity or integrity.
Origin of *HEAL:* Middle English *helen,* from Old English
hǣlan; akin to Old High German *heilen,* to heal, Old English
hāl whole—more at whole
—*Merriam-Webster dictionary*

From this definition, it's clear that heal is an action, something to be done by you or for you. The origin of the word,
which dates back to before the twelfth century, means
"more at whole." My mission is to help you become more
whole and heal the internal holes by filling them. When we
do this, we become whole once again, just as we were
when we first arrived here on this planet.

The heal component of the spiral is about awareness
and recognition. When you become aware of what needs
to be addressed in your life, you are able to recognize the
parts inside of you that need to heal in order for you to
grow. That's why I spoke first about the concept of feel.
You must have an awareness of your inner world. It is like
opening your eyes just a little wider than usual and seeing
more clearly what you need to know about yourself. With
this clear vision, you can begin the process of internally
recognizing what you need to address and tend to in order
to heal. In order to address it, you must first recognize it
within the self.

What do you know about how to heal, feel better, take care of yourself? What are the first steps you can take? Healing takes place one piece, one strand, one part, one level at a time. Healing is an ever-evolving process, because we are each infinite and ever-evolving.

To be on the continuum of the spiral is to let yourself feel it out. It is like when you walk into a dark room and all you can sense is your feet on the floor, so you carefully step into the dark, slowly feeling your way around, taking baby steps, trusting and knowing that, at some point, you will find the light switch. Entering the spiral with the intention to heal is like walking into the dark room. You are entering a place of trust within yourself. You are the one in charge of your path of healing as you travel the layers of the spiral. When you ask what is needed to heal, what this part of the spiral asks you is, *What is needed to heal?* You have gifts inside that will allow your healing to happen. Do not look outside of yourself. Do not seek from others what you need to be said in order for you to feel better. That is not healing, it is a Band-Aid.

Healing is the greatest gift of self-love. Healing is a rising from within, an awareness that you must be responsible for taking care of yourself. My definition of healing is: "sifting through the layers of pain within and addressing the hurt with the intention to help the hurt transform." The goal is to transform that place of pain within us to a place that is loved, that can feel the love, and that is able to know it is loved. In the end, isn't that what all of us want: love?

What I want you to remember about healing is that you are in control when it comes to how much healing you are going to do in this life. Not merely to survive or go through but to heal. It is within the space inside yourself where you tap into your strengths and grow, heal, become. You must first create a safe space for this to happen. You create this space by being present, letting go of expectations, and allowing life to unfold without reaction but instead with a deep respect for the unfolding of it all so that you can respond from wholeness and not react from brokenness.

We can survive a trauma, but we then need to heal from it in order to make ourselves once again whole. To be at a place within our self that redefines what being whole means. For healing to happen, you will be called forward to allow yourself to go through and experience a full range of feelings and emotions, and doing so requires that you be very brave. To feel the feelings, you need to sit in and with the feelings, be present with them.

When I work with clients to heal their traumas through hypnotherapy, we look at the experiences from a place of safety. Healing is not the reliving of a trauma. Healing is gaining an understanding that in that time of pain, at the age you were, you did the best you could with the resources you had in that moment to survive. You learn that you can let go of those old beliefs, fears, emotions, and patterns because they are no longer working for you in your present life. You transform the pain by transforming your perceptions of the experience.

Each of us develops coping skills based on our perceptions of a situation, not the actual reality of the situation. When you go back and look at it with the wisdom of your loving adult self, you can understand how, at that earlier time, you perceived it the way that you did and developed the coping skills necessary to survive. As I have said before, the deeper mind has no sense of time, so it does not know that it is many years or even a week later. It is stuck. That is why, in my opinion, healing needs to happen at a cellular level. Not only in the mind, because the mind is limited but also in the body, through the chakras where the emotional energy has been stored.

People work really hard to avoid the big pieces of pain they carry within. When you spend a lot of energy avoiding your pain, you miss the opportunities that show up in order to allow you a way to heal. When you are avoiding your deep feelings, you are proving to yourself the false belief that you do not love yourself enough to heal. The limiting belief that you cannot love yourself because intrinsically, hidden way down deep, in a place that you don't like to look at or acknowledge, is a place that does not feel worthy of love and, therefore, healing. When people don't feel worthy of love, they over-identify with those pieces that are not lovable. If you do not work on yourself and the hurt inner child that lives inside of you, you will continue to recreate the same pattern. The pattern will show up until you are ready to learn from it and heal. It is almost unavoidable.

These recreated patterns are self-sabotage. You have

likely heard this action discussed or had friends ask you whether you were self-sabotaging, ruining a good thing? Why do you always pick the same type of partner? Why do you regain the same ten pounds over and over again each time you lose it? These patterns are going to keep showing up until you see them and heal the one inside of you who is creating them. The havoc that is created is not created to cause you pain. It is created so that the inner child who is in pain can get your attention. That little one needs help but does not know how to get it. It only knows how to function in a dysfunctional way in this area of your life. It does not matter if the dysfunction shows itself as an issue of weight, relationships, career, money, or challenges with children. It will keep showing up until you pause long enough to say, "I am going to take care of you now. I am ready to love you, because you are lovable. I am ready to go there, to the source of the pain, to look at it, to unravel it and heal it."

Once you do that, you will no longer need to look to the outside for the validation of your own self-worth. That validation will come from the inside. When we look to another for love, we are looking to them to make us feel whole. If your child comes to you with words such as "I hate you," you feel deeply hurt and insulted because, intrinsically, these words are taken in as truth. The belief systems in place are "I do not feel lovable" and "It makes sense that you hate me because, secretly, I hate myself." In that moment, you do not feel you are enough, worthy, or lovable and you over-identify with the pieces inside that are injured.

Our children, especially, are showing us a mirror of our damaged self that needs to heal. We all walk around unconscious, and we must heal in order not to project our pain onto others. It is important to point out that all projections and judgements you have about others (or that others have about you) really reflect the way you (or they) feel about yourself (or they feel about themselves). Let's take an example. Think about what happens when someone gives you a compliment. Are you able to easily say, "Thank you"? Many of us are not. We instead have to justify the compliment. If someone says, "I love your sweater," instead of saying, "Thank you" and moving on, we have to justify it by saying something along the lines of, "Oh this, I got it for five dollars at a discount store." We then minimize our self even more and prove to our self, with our words, that we are not worthy of a mere compliment.

When you answer another in this way, it serves as greater proof both to yourself and from yourself that the belief system in place is accurate. When you can say, "Thank you," it shows deep self-care. Just say, "Thank you" when someone gives you a compliment; stop apologizing for yourself. When you do, you begin to change the story attached to the faulty belief system. There is nothing to apologize for. There is no one-size-fits-all prescription as to what you can do for yourself, to feel and fuel yourself, to allow your heart to feel something, to feel calm, to have self-awareness.

My favorite metaphor when it comes to understanding healing and what happens when we heal with transformational hypnotherapy involves an onion. Healing involves peeling layers like those on an onion, especially when doing hypnosis. Think about it. When you peel an onion, sometimes you work really hard just to get off the super thin layers. It makes you absolutely crazy, it takes a long time and is frustrating and painful. If it is a really strong onion, you find yourself crying. Your eyes start to burn so much, and you only removed the thinnest layer of skin, which required so much work. At these times, you need to take a break, wash your hands, clean the mascara off your face, and breathe before you can go back to work peeling that layer of the onion. At other times, you can peel the onion and easily get off a big piece of the skin. It comes right off without hurting at all. This is what happens when we heal. Sometimes the layers we are peeling are painful, and they come off slowly and with a lot of tears and work. Other times, what we are dealing with is easier to go through and process, so we easily get a large layer off the onion. But, no matter what, we keep peeling the onion because we need to. Without it, the particular meal we desire to cook would be bland. We need to peel it back and look at the pain. You see, those painful layers get in the way of living a rich and complete life. Keeping those layers of the onion, thick or thin, block you from living to your full potential. Those painful layers are blocking your light.

When you go back to the Spiral of Healing, with each

184 • JANET PHILBIN

layer you go up, you are taking off another layer of the onion. We are touching the layers over and over again, but at different intensities. Each time we move up a level of the Spiral of Healing, we look at it the pain with a new perspective and look at a different aspect of it.

To give you another way to think about it, I will use myself as an example. A few months back, as I was pedaling away in my spin class, a thought popped into my head. This thought was "I better push harder because I am fat." I heard this thought and caught it immediately. I knew I needed to change that sentence. I instantly changed it to "I am able to push harder because I am strong." This was a much more empowering, motivating, and true sentence. What struck me in that moment was how easily this negative, untrue sentence casually wound up in my train of thought. If I had not caught it, I could have spun out of control emotionally while I was spinning on my bike. I was glad I caught it and found an immediate replacement sentence. I think this is an important skill we all need to learn as we heal.

It is time to begin to listen closely, to change the sentences, and change the thoughts. Instead of saying to yourself, "I need to do this because I'm fat or ugly or lazy," begin to change your self-talk to "I am doing this because I am strong, worthy, healthy, and important." The language we use to talk to our self is important. As we heal, we become more conscious and aware of our self-talk and can catch ourselves more quickly. I am asking you to pay attention to the words you use when you think about yourself. When you catch yourself in negative thoughts, stop for a moment and restate your sentence with a positive affirmation.

The negative self-talk comes from the ego, and they are the words of the inner child. These are the words that may have been said to us by people in our lives as we grew up. Or, they may have been the words you used to hear the adults in your life say about themselves. Either way, this kind of negative self-talk became internalized and then identified with as someone or something that you are. These thoughts live in your head and show up when you are in self-judgement. They also appear when you feel scared, uncertain, not worthy, depressed, shame, anger, disempowered, guilt, self-deprecating, and any other painful emotion you can think of. It is important for your authentic self and voice to show up when this kind of self-talk comes in.

When you begin to recognize the need to feel positive, empowered, and inspired you hear the call to self-care. The call to begin to see and feel your intrinsic value.

When you begin to change your self-talk, language, and thoughts, you let your inner child know that he is seen, heard, worthy, and important. That he matters. It is important to pay attention to the language you are using. Begin by using the words "I am." *I am strong, I am empowered, I am worthy.* Then, create a new sentence with "I am *because* I am strong," "I am meditating *because* I am grounded and connected to oneness energy," "I am creating *because* what I have to offer the world is needed by humankind."

Pay attention to the self-talk, listen to the language your thinking mind is using and correct yourself when necessary. The thinking mind is not enlightened. The thinking mind functions in the form-based world. This means the world view is limited by only the things you can see and touch. Do you allow yourself to tap into the formless energy and acknowledge that the energy is abundant, flowing, and rich? The formless is in our belief system that there is more out there than that which we can see, touch, and hear. It is our trust in the universe. When you can trust in the formless energy of the universe, you are in flow and abundance.

This abundant energy is there for you, so let's practice these exercises to change the negative self-talk. In changing the self-talk, you are doing healing. Change the self-deprecating words to positive, empowering, allowing, and inspiring words. Begin using "I am" in your sentences, and notice the difference it makes.

Here are some steps you can take to care for your emotions in the moment when your pain rises up within you. They can be done individually, or you can combine a few at a time. Take what you need, apply it in your life, and create the room for you to feel and heal.

- Positive self-talk
- Meditate
- Feel it

- Acknowledge it
- Have patience for self
- Do not be harsh of critical of self

When you practice the above skills, you are bringing yourself into a place of wholeness. You have it in you to recognize the holes and come back to a place of wholeness. When you feel yourself about to go over the edge, remember that you are in control of you. No one else can do for you what you are most able to do for yourself. Here are four steps that can bring you back from the emotional edge.

Meditate
Set the time aside for yourself to focus on your breath, be present, and allow the feelings to rise up, flow through you, be, and let go. Ask yourself, "What kind of pain am I in?"

Talk
Talk to someone who is safe, who gets it, and who can hold and honor the emotional space you are in without judgement. This is important, because when we are in a place of vulnerability, being judged will not feel safe. It will only further disempower you.

Exercise
This will get you back in touch with your body. If you can, get outside to exercise in nature. Being outside will help

ground you and connect you even more deeply to the present moment.

Journal
Journal about these steps you can take to begin to help yourself find your holes and become whole again.

Doing these four things will help you get out of the thinking mind and back into your heart space, back to feeling whole.

We do not want fear to shut the door to our abundance and healing. That door is one we want to keep wide open. The way to do that is to remove the fear. The only way to remove fear is to feel it, listen to it, honor it, learn from it, and help it release.

GROW

Grow: *verb*: To spring up and develop to maturity. To be able to grow in some place or situation. To increase in wisdom. To promote the development of.
—*Merriam-Webster dictionary*

Allow me to begin this section with an insight I received as I was looking to understand what it means for me to grow and how I was to understand the process in my own life.

Your truth is the truth that lies within each one of us as we shed the old and embrace the new. The shedding of the old is a process that requires some pain, because without the pain there can be no growth. Without the growth, we cannot blossom into the new flower we are becoming. Allow the pain, and allow yourself to blossom, as everyone is blossoming right along with you, over and over again. Be in the love of all that is eternal, the knowing that comes from within a soul that cries out. It is time to be heard. Do not turn your back on the growth that is within you. Look inside for beauty and truth, not outside. The gifts lie within you.

It is up to you to trust in your heart and in the wisdom that you are being given. It is through this trust that you allow space for the self and true growth to emerge. When you close your eyes and look inward, you are able to see more of your truth and your essence. When the eyes are closed, you are able to move from the external world of looking out and comparison to the internal world of looking in, feeling and experiencing only that which you can know to be true about yourself while tapping into the source energy that is within you. The outside world cannot offer you the truth and the answers you seek. The outside world offers judgements and comparisons. Your inner world offers you your truth of knowing. And, in finding the truth of your inner knowing, you allow space to grow.

My definition of grow is: "a process of breaking free." Once you can break free, the ability to become is vast and full of potential. To grow is to put down the heavy bags you have been carrying. To grow allows for an expansion of your conscious awareness for healing and emotional wellness. To grow means to move up the Spiral of Healing a little bit at a time. Do not be afraid of growth, as that which is in front of you offers you the path to emotional freedom.

Ask yourself, "What do I need to break free from?" We do not need to grow in big chunks; we can grow in small, bite-sized pieces. When you bite off more than you can chew, you set yourself up to fail. The goal in your growth is forward movement on your path. Another goal to keep in mind as you grow is, remember to stay calm when you find yourself in the storms of life. When you tap into your own inner landscape and can be the peace that is within you, you are tapping into one of your greatest strengths. And this strength brings you the opportunity to grow and become.

When I talk about growth and growing, I want to talk about it from the place of our personal power center. Let's focus on the solar plexus chakra for a moment. The solar plexus chakra is my favorite, because it is our power center. It is the compass rose that points me in the right direction on the path to my goals in life. There may be obstacles on this path—some of these may be large obstacles, some small and easy to manage. One thing I have learned over the past thirty years of my healing journey is that if I am patient with myself and with my process, the way through the obstacles will eventually show itself. When I am solid and strong in my solar plexus, I imagine a Native American woman standing there, very tall, with her spear in hand, looking forward, looking out onto the path, trusting in her heart that she has all she needs inside of her to make it to the end of the path. Knowing she can make it to her new self, the one who has healed, who has grown, who has accomplished her goals and is ready to begin a new journey.

The path to healing and growth is not straight. In fact, it is usually quite crooked. There are also no shortcuts along it; trust me, I wish there were. The way to grow and heal is to go through. As I tell my clients, there is no going around, over, or under; we must go through. Sometimes, what you must go through looks pretty dark as you approach it. It may seem like you have to enter the darkest of tunnels, not knowing where or when it will end. The moment of stepping forward into the tunnel is the moment you must have the greatest trust in yourself. The moment you access the warrior of your solar plexus, bang your spear on the ground, and step forward is your invitation to become. You step forward because you know the only way to grow in this area of your life is to go through the pain of dealing with whatever is in that dark tunnel. While in the tunnel, you grow through your pain. You grow *because* of your pain. You grow because your pain is there to help you, to teach you, and to allow you to evolve into a new version of yourself--one who can love the self and feel worthy, enough, and important.

When you exit the tunnel, you will find the light. The light was always waiting for you, you were just too afraid to enter and go through to the other side. But it was there the whole time. When you arrive into the light, you will be free and embraced for your bravery. You will feel proud and more confident. It is just like when the sky is overcast, and we cannot see the sun. The sun is still shining, we just cannot see it through the clouds. There is a level of trust you need to have in yourself and in the guidance you are being given when you enter the tunnel. Granted, we do not know how long the journey will take, but if you are brave enough to persevere, you will come through to the other side, standing taller, having grown. You will be ready to move up the spiral to another level, a new level of awareness and healing.

I believe that all of us come here to have a human experience for our spiritual learning. When the human learning matches the soul's truth, it is like two pieces of a puzzle fitting together. It is at this point that we can reach a place of transcendence to understand our self from the wisdom of the soul, which is limitless, as opposed to the wisdom of humanity, which has limits. We cannot be in this place all of the time. It is a place we touch, feel, and come back from only to touch again. We live in the world of form, and the transcendent place is formless. However, when you can access the transcendent and touch the formless, you will have a knowing of what is there for you by how you feel, by what you sense, by what you come to intuitively know. You can then manifest it in the form-based world. Much as I am manifesting this book right now, before I put these words on the page, they were formless. No one was able to know them before they were written. As it comes together, it becomes form. Writing this book is part of my growth, and it has been years in the making. As I grow through the writing of it, I am feeling many things. I am in a place of self-love because I am doing something for me that is coming from me and is something I care about deeply. Due to all of this, I heal even more layers of my own onion. I rise up on the spiral.

Now, of course not all growth comes from writing a book. It can happen in a therapy session, while you journal, meditate, pray, walk, or during any other activity where you are looking inward in order to understand yourself.

One goal is to allow yourself to come into the knowing of the unknown. To enter the emotional freedom that is there for you. All of us long to be free, healed, and healthy. We are all beings who can offer freedom to the self. There are no blocks to your growth potential. There are many stairs, but it is up to you to choose which ones to climb, how to climb them, and how high to go. The potential for growth is limitless. Are you willing to touch your limitless potential?

There is also no room for self-doubt if there is to be growth. Does your self-doubt hold you back? Self-doubt is usually fear-based. When you are doubting your ability, questioning whether or not you are able to do, accomplish, or attempt something, it is time to look inside and see what the fear is about and where you are holding it. Which chakra is the fear living in? Once you can identify the fear, deconstruct it, and understand why it was there

194 • JANET PHILBIN

and how it came to be, you will be able to heal it and grow from there.

Doubt slows you down and gets in the way of you growing into who you are truly meant to be. The false beliefs about self that are based on programming from your life take over. The false self will continue to influence us until we heal those parts, those parts represented by fear. They are the voices of self-doubt that run through our mind daily. We learned these things based on different experiences in life, and we bought into them as being true. I am here to confirm for you that these thoughts are not who you are. As Michael Singer says in his book, *The Untethered Soul*, "We are not our thoughts." This is a very powerful concept to understand, begin to believe, and embrace. If you wish to transform out of self-doubt and lack-based thinking and into abundant, expansive, limitless-potential-based feelings, you must pull the cover off of self-doubt and expose it for what it really is.

Self-doubt is a thief of the true essence of the empowered and enlightened self.

Do not be fooled or misled into believing the lies of the false self. They can be seductive at times, seducing you into believing in them as a way to keep you feeling that you are safe, when quite the opposite is true. Believing them keeps you stuck—not growing, not expanding, not becoming. It is time to begin to look inside and find your voice, find your true self, get in touch with your essence, and call out the lies of the false self. This is how you reprogram your beliefs and heal. As this happens, you will find a decrease in anxiety, an increase in focus, clearer thinking, and less of a feeling of being easily frazzled. When you do feel frazzled, you will be able to come back to center more quickly. You will be more confident in yourself and your abilities, and trust in your potential to create for yourself the life you want. I ask you to flow into it, flow with it, do not fight what is there inside you. Nurture yourself to make space for that which is ready to break free. It is time for growth and transformation.

Allow wisdom to flow through you. Sit with it. There is no need to think, judge, or wonder. Just allow and behold all that can come. It will unfold; it *is* unfolding. You will continue to learn and be guided toward helpers for your growth. There are also people out there who need *your* perspective and wisdom. Pause here for a moment to look back and see all the stepping stones you needed to walk on to get here. Would you have picked up a book like this a year ago or five years ago? Something led you here, and I'd propose that it was you. It was your longing to know more, to grow more, to heal more. Pause again, look forward, and see the stepping stones that will take you into the future. See your own inner warrior, who stands on his/her path looking out, setting the intention to reach the next part of the journey on the spiral to heal. The path has been cleared by the manifestation intention you just set. Go forward bravely. There is support around you.

Journal Prompts

- What has kept you "encaged"?

- Why have you been so afraid that you have made a choice to stay stuck?

- Where in your body do you feel these feelings that have kept you stuck? In which chakra do they sit? How do they look? Describe them.

- In your imagination, what do they need in order to heal and grow?

No one can answer these questions for you. They must come from you. Take a breath, close your eyes, ask yourself the questions, be in the feelings, experience the feelings, identify them, write them down.

LOVE

Love: *noun*: Strong affection for another arising out of kinship or personal ties; maternal *love* for a child; attraction based on sexual desire, affection, and tenderness felt by lovers; affection based on admiration, benevolence, or common interests; an assurance of affection
—*Merriam-Webster dictionary*

How do we define love? How can we begin to understand it? We hear terms and phrases like "true love," "romantic love," "being in love," "love for a child," "love for a pet," and "love for the Earth." I am sure you can name even more. There have been books written about the languages of love, couples and love, and self-love as well as many children's books about love—what it means and how it looks—love and attachment, love and religion, and unconditional love.

When I talk about love with regard to the Spiral of Healing, I am speaking of the importance of learning to love yourself for who you are, as you are. For accepting yourself—lumps, bumps, and all—because you are perfect; there is nothing to fix. There are only experiences that are in need of healing. There is a starting point within each of us where we come to learn that emotional freedom is attainable through healing. When we come from a place of self-love, we are at the starting line of becoming who we are truly meant to be. When we pause we remember that, in order to heal, we must love our self, and that in the loving of self, we begin to learn what it is within us that really needs our attention. Meditation is a way to be on the path to heal and get to know one's true self. Below is a poem I wrote a while back about love and healing.

IT IS ALL WITHIN YOU

Do not be afraid of all that is still to be uncovered.
Where is the truth that lies within?

Does it hide in the shadows of the mind?
The truth is what whispers to you, the longing of your soul.
You hear the answers through feelings and synchronicities.
There is no love if there is no light.
The peace must rise up from within in order to bloom into form.
It is all within you, open the door to let it in.
Do not falter, love the self, love the self, love the self.

When I wrote this, I had begun to more deeply understand that it was time for me to step out of my shadows. To shine the light within me in order to find and see my truth. And to know that finding my truth means only that I have to look inside. That my soul always knows this truth, and so does yours. As we open to the truth of our soul, we open to the ability to love the self. This is where we are being guided—to loving the self. When we love the self, we can be in abundance of that love and have overflow to share with another.

The way I define love for the process of healing is "a sense of self-acceptance, a sense of inner calm, an inner knowing that you are okay just as you are in this moment in time." It is a deep self-caring. It's the place within which you know you can trust yourself above all else. We can only love another as much as we love our self. We can only *receive* love from another to the degree that we love our self. Loving the self is the integral piece.

Further, it cannot be a false love. It cannot be a love formed out of ego but one formed from seeing that you are valuable, worthy, and important. You must see in yourself these qualities.

You are the one in charge of your own letting go. When you let go, you free yourself. It's an empowering choice. It's saying to yourself, "I love you. I value you as I choose to let go of all I have held that has hurt me."

We cannot freely share with another if we are feeling depleted. From the place of a depleted heart, we may be in resistance to love. Our heart may be very defensive, and we therefore protect it. If we are defensive and protective, we will resist letting love in from another as well as letting love into our own hearts from ourselves. This may sound confusing and leave you wondering, *How do I let love into my own heart from me*? Allow me to explain.

We each have the ability to tap into the love that is in our hearts. Your love is already inside of you, and when you access your heart light, you have the ability to send love to a part of you, to the part within that is in pain. I would like you to pause here for a moment and do a brief exercise with me. Take a breath, and as you do, place your hand over your heart. Bring to mind the most recent time you were upset about something. Once you can recall that time, take another breath, feel your palm over your heart, and imagine that you can scan your body and allow yourself to feel where in your body are you responding to your feelings. Is it your stomach, shoulders, head? Wherever it is, use your imagination and imagine your own heart is a beautiful healing light. You can shine your heart light like the rays of the sun to the part of your body that is feeling this discomfort and soothe it, love it, ease it, and allow that discomfort to ease up and feel better. Keep sending the light to this part until it begins to shift, until it begins to feel even more comfortable. As you do this, be mindful that you are also holding your own heart. Feel your heart, as this allows you to connect even more deeply with yourself. You see, you are not alone within you; you have yourself.

The light of your heart can be directed anywhere by you at any time. You have that ability within you always—the power to tune in with your breath and send your own loving light out to wherever you need it, whenever you need it. This is your own personal superpower. This is what I mean when I say, "Let love into your own heart from yourself." You are the most powerful participant in your own healing when you can imagine sending heart light to your own heart or any other part of you that is holding emotional pain.

One of my hypnotherapy clients had just this problem—the problem of not knowing how to be loving and compassionate with himself. Leroy is a man in his thirties with two daughters under the age of eight. He came to see me because he knew he was projecting his own anxieties onto his children but did not know why and did not know how to stop. He would become easily frustrated with his daughters and became quite reactive when they did something he perceived as wrong, like speaking too loudly or eating in a sloppy manner. He was always over-correcting his daughters and being critical. As I worked with Leroy during his hypnosis sessions, we accessed his feelings through tuning into his body and his chakras.

What we came to learn was that, as a young boy, in order to protect himself, he built a big box around his heart. This box had energetically been in place since he was ten years old. As a ten-year-old boy, he decided that he was not good enough, did not feel worthy, was not liked, and needed to be careful about who he trusted. He sometimes did not feel loved, important, or cared about.

As you can imagine, having a big box around your heart for almost thirty years can do a lot of emotional damage, even though the box was originally placed there to protect him. We had to help the ten-year-old who placed the box there learn that he did not need it anymore. The ten-year-old needed to learn that Leroy had grown up. He was now a successful business owner, a husband, and a father who was surrounded by love. Through the healing process I use when I work with clients, Leroy was able to first find the box. Once found, we were able to work with ten-year-old Leroy to understand what was going on in that little boy's life at the time when he decided that, in order to cope and survive, this box had to be put in place. This box served a purpose. It kept him safe and protected. In order to re-move the box, we had to inform the ten-year-old that he survived. We had to tell young Leroy that adult Leroy was able to understand why, at ten, he felt the way that he did, and we knew that he did the best he could at that time in order to cope and survive. We spoke to the ten-year-old and let him know that it was now safe to feel love from the adult self. Once ten-year-old Leroy felt better, because he was understood and forgiven for the impact of the box, he agreed that he did not need to keep it anymore, that it was finished serving a purpose in adult Leroy's life. An important part of the healing was in using Leroy's heart light while we tapped into universal light and love, the love that is available for all of us, and filling that box with love, light, and healing.

This was the beginning of the healing transformation for Leroy. In following sessions, we continued to work with his heart and self-love, and we were eventually able to remove the box completely, which enabled him to be in a place of love for himself without the lack-based feelings he previously had. Without those lack-based feelings, he no longer needed to project them onto his daughters. There were many aspects of these feelings, based on various life experiences he'd had. I can tell you that by our last session, his reactivity was almost gone, his insight had improved tremendously, he was able to have more fun with his children, and he was meditating and journaling regularly. He had neither meditated nor journaled before that, and he learned that the more he let love in, the more he was able to be in the feeling of joy, to experience love, and to allow himself the freedoms of being, of loving himself, and of being loved by others.

It is also important that we take some time to explore the greatest barriers to self-love. In my opinion, the greatest barrier to self-love is the belief that we hold deep down inside that we are not lovable, not worthy, not enough. Underneath all of the pain and the suffering lie these beliefs, which were learned many years ago and continue to manifest in present-day life. They may show up as an inability to commit to your own self-care. The internal pain feels too big to touch. This may lead to externalizing responsibility and blaming another person. When it is the other's fault, you do not have to look at your own pain and feelings of unworthiness.

Perhaps you are always chasing another's love. This may show up as insecurity with the need to prove oneself. It may show up when you are constantly and consistently putting someone else's needs in front of your own. It shows up in the feeling that taking care of them is more important than your own self-care.

Self-care is self-love. When you take time out for self-care, it is a way of showing self-love. I am not referring to activities such as manicures and massages. Those are nice, but they are also external. I am talking about taking time out to do the things that fuel your soul—taking a walk in nature, reading a good book, meditating, eating healthy foods, exercising because it is good for you, journaling, singing, or being creative in any way. We are so busy "doing" that we do not take the time to just "be."

Being is self-care. Being in stillness, being in silence, being without the use of an electronic device that only distracts you from your being state. Allowing yourself the space and time for creativity is self-care. Creativity comes from being in the flow with the internal and external energy. When you block the internal or external energy, you block creativity. Creativity fuels life, and without it we become depressed. We were meant to create. This is how the species has survived and flourished, by allowing the imagination to lead the way.

Using your imagination is self-care. In the flow of creativity, you are honoring yourself and your authentic voice. When we follow the gifts that are sparked by imagination, it allows the energy to flow into and through the creative places inside of us that give voice to the creative self. Do not block the voice of creativity because you are scared, uncertain, or afraid of others' reactions. There is a special spark that came through you, in order for you to bring the idea/creation to humanity. There are those who create, and there those who are the receivers of others' creations. Be a creator, and as you create, know that you are loving yourself. Let your own unique voice be heard. You have so much to offer.

Have you ever given thought to what blocks you from being in a state of being? What prevents you from being who you truly are? What is blocking you from self-love? In order to be, you need to accept the as-is of your state of being as well as others' states of being. That means fully accepting your reality in the moment, because in that moment, it is what it is. It cannot be another way until you move into the next moment. There are desires underneath the surface that interrupt our ability to be in the flow of being, to allow space for self-love, and to be in the moment as it is. Desires that look outside of the self include:

- the desire of what others need and want you to be; something other than who you are
- the desire of what you want and need others to be; something other than who they are

These desires are the source of our pain. We fight the reality of accepting what is in front of us and instead go into pain. We attach a story to the pain and fight reality because we are always looking to find validation to hold onto the story in our minds. Maybe you need to hold onto the belief that you are right. What would it mean to let go of these beliefs?

In order to stay attached to our beliefs, we will project, rationalize, and justify our story. Getting stuck in the desire to have something outside of us change and fighting the as-is keeps us stuck in a circle that will get us nowhere except spinning our wheels. This will leave us feeling frustrated, upset, and unheard; or unloved, unvalidated, or unseen. However, we do this to ourselves because we are not practicing self-care and the art of being. Here is a graphic to help clarify the concept:

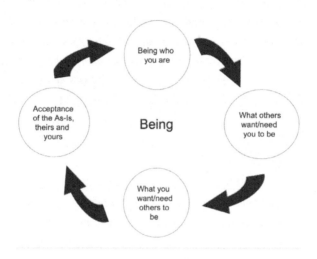

Can you see how easy it is to get stuck in this cycle? How looking outside of you toward others pulls you away from your own state of being? One of the goals is not to be distracted by thoughts. The thoughts and the stories about the thoughts are just another way to keep you from being. It is important to be aware of this, because all of us fall prey to comparison and wanting to be what another person needs. In a way, we cannot help it. We were programmed this way in childhood in order to survive. Beliefs came to be developed as we learned who we needed to be or become in the eyes of our primary caregivers in order to be loved, get our needs met, or maybe even survive. This is where and how the ego developed. As we become conscious that we are not in our being state, that we are not in a place of self-love, we can look to this circle and ask yourself if we are wanting others to change and be a certain way for *us*. Are we "trying" to change in order to be a certain way for another? Are we fighting the as-is of our current reality, and in fighting this reality, adding to our own discomfort and emotional upset in the present moment? As we bring our awareness to these aspects of our thoughts, we are becoming more mindful. And, in becoming more mindful, we will be able to catch ourselves and bring ourselves back to present-moment awareness. When we are in this place of being, we are in a place of self-love.

It is in the journey that you find your voice. Your awareness is growing. Life lessons are the cornerstones, the building blocks, to greater awareness of the soul. To be means to be in and with your feelings, especially at the times when the feelings are the most uncomfortable. When you are uncomfortable with anxious feelings, you look to take action. The action-taking is a release, like opening a valve to let out steam. But, when this is done, you then have learned nothing new, only experienced a relearning of the old. To be is to tolerate the pressure of being uncomfortable and allow it to be felt, then to dissipate. To call in support, to not fix, to learn to be comfortable in the discomfort, to stay with it until the discomfort becomes comfortable again. The place inside that feels uncomfortable will become comfortable again as you sit in it. Then you will learn that you are in control of feelings of anxiety, fear, and lack of control. Don't let them control you. Be in it in order to allow the full range of emotion. To accept that moment of the journey. To embrace what you have learned and your growth from being. It is all within you. Do not be afraid. There are more lessons coming your way. Some will be difficult. You will learn to use your voice to express your truth, to face fears, to venture out.

Much of this insight has already come to pass in my own life. I have had great challenges, and in moving through those challenges, I had to learn to *be* with extremely uncomfortable feelings. The other truth that has come to be is that, since 2016, I have learned how to use my voice to express my truth. In writing this book and sharing so much of my process, I am venturing out of my safe, small world and not letting my fears stop me. Occupying your being state is powerful, transformative, and healing.

A way to come back to self-love and being in the moment is to sit in silence and hear your own breath, even if only for five minutes. This is really a gift that you give yourself. A few more ways to come back to self-love are to get enough sleep each night and to connect with others who know your heart, those who you do not need to be fake with and have small talk with about nonsense.

When you hear the term self-love, do you think about

all of the misconceptions widely held by society. A big misconception many hold about self-love is that it is egoic, in the Western psychology sense of ego—one who is full of himself. Self-love is not from ego. Self-love comes from your own heart. There is so much wisdom that the heart holds. When you open up your heart or yourself to the wisdom of your heart, you can access all of your gifts and abilities. In your heart space, there is no ego, there is no judgement, there is no anger, jealousy, or shame. The truth of your heart is pure. Anything negative you feel is not coming from the space of the heart; it's coming from ego, which is the false self, the wounded one inside spoken about in chapter 2. This ego has no place in the heart, but it does not know where else to go because you are hurting and it still believes it needs to protect you in some way. If it keeps you "small" with feelings of unworthiness, you stay stuck and will have a very hard time being able to be in a place of self-love and self-care.

In essence, you suffer when you are in your ego. You heal when you are in your heart. You can transform the pages in your life when you allow the self to step aside of your ego and into the messages of your heart. The heart has the ability to tap into its own wisdom. Will you have days where you are not in your heart wisdom? Of course. Do not forget that you are a spiritual being having a human experience. You will be in the reactivity of your humanity at times, for it is impossible not to be. When that happens, be kind to and forgiving of yourself. Allow room to have insight, look at your emotions, and above all, have self-compassion. If you can be loving and open for another, you must also be able to be loving and open for yourself.

Do you know that you are abundant, worthy and enough? I find that people are afraid to say they love who they are, even if they do. This kind of self-love is not often shared because there is worry about judgement from another. In day-to-day conversation, people would think you were from Mars if you openly professed to love yourself. I mean, who goes around saying they love themselves? Only those who are pompous, right? I believe this is where we have gone in the wrong direction.

If you can be in a place of self-love, you are in a place of self-acceptance, warts and all. When and why did we learn that it was not okay to like or love the self? Why were we taught to always put another first? Most of us were taught that if we put another first, it shows that we are a good person, have good values, and are caring. If this is what society has taught us, that must mean that taking good care of yourself first is bad and somehow wrong. But I must ask, if you do not take care of you and love you first, who will? In order to feel you are lovable by others, you must first feel you are able to be loved by yourself. If you cannot love yourself, find yourself worthy and important, you will always be chasing love on the outside. As I have already shared, there is nothing on the outside that will heal your inner holes. Healing on all levels is inside-out work.

Another place you can start is through the language you use when you speak about yourself. When you think or speak about yourself, what are the first words you hear? If you had to describe yourself to someone else, what words would you use? If you were asked whether or not you liked yourself, what would you say? If you were asked whether or not you loved yourself, what would you say? Think about how you answered these questions. Did you use positive or negative words? The first step in putting self-love into action in a way whereby you can make small changes on the journey to full self-love is to pay attention to the language you are using.

Words have an energy and a vibration. When words are thought about and then spoken, they carry an energy with them. The positive carry a positive energy, and the negative carry a negative energy. What if you began to replace negative self-talk with positive words and thoughts? When you change your words, you change your vibration. You then create space to experience the world and who you are in the world in a new way. You create space for abundance and positivity and make room for self-care.

If you go back to the purposeful pause, we spoke about in chapter 9, you can empower yourself to change your self-expression. In the pause, you take a breath and change the thought and the words before you speak them. Pause here with me for a minute. Let me ask again the questions I asked previously. This time, only describe your feelings about yourself with positive words.

Journal Prompts

- When you think about yourself, what are the first words you hear?

- Describe yourself to someone else.

- If you were asked if you liked and loved yourself what would you say?

- Are you able to change the words?

- Did you notice a difference in how you felt?

Each small move you make in your approach to daily life in your words to yourself allows for your healing, growth, and manifestation. Experiment with this each day, and take note of how you begin to feel.

The love that you seek is the love that you are.

This is the truth. I believe that when we are born, we become separated from source energy, and we come to learn and believe that we cannot touch it again. When we cannot touch, feel, and experience something, it is hard for us to know it is true. A big forgetting happens, and we become seekers of that which we already truly are: love. As humans we are always looking for proof. Heck, if I cannot find it in a Google search, it must not be a real thing, right? Where is the validation coming from?

How can you validate love from the outside? Can anyone really tell you what love feels like inside of you? No, they cannot. Do you know why? Because your feelings are *your* feelings, and the way you experience those feelings is unique to you. That is why comparison to others always leaves us lacking, and in those experiences, we somehow wind up falling short. When you can embrace this idea that the love that you seek on the outside is actually the love that you already are on the inside, you are growing and healing.

You were born with all of the gifts of self-love. You are able to take care of and nurture yourself. I am asking you not to turn away from your truth and your true essence.

Instead, I ask that you turn *toward* your heart. Allow yourself to look inside and find what has been waiting there for you all along.

How do you get there, how do you become the love that you are? How does this become a living, active part of you? Because we are conditioned to believe that self-love is selfish, it is a new practice for us to embrace the idea that it isn't. What if we shifted this paradigm and reframed it to one whereby when you are taking care of yourself? When you are loving yourself and doing activities and spending time with yourself in ways that honor your truth, that are in alignment with who you really are, you are making yourself sacred. You deserve to be sacred. It is okay to begin to change your belief system about self-love from selfish to sacred. You are a sacred human being who came here to be the love that you are and to share that love without expectations.

Here are a few of my personal tips and strategies for engaging in self-love. I don't do chores after 8pm. I get in my PJs early, especially when the days are shorter and I don't have to go out again. I sit down and drink a cup of tea. I read. I make meditation and journaling a priority. I exercise regularly. I limit my TV watching, especially the news. I also enjoy doing something mindless. Here is my big confession: I am shamelessly addicted to Candy Crush. People think that I don't do this kind of mindless game playing, but I do. I am human, just like you, and we all need down time and a way to relax and take a little time-out in order to allow our brain not to think. That is okay.

Spend ten to thirty minutes letting yourself unwind each day.

I recently decided to experiment and see if I could take a break from Candy Crush. I was going to journal about all the things I could get done without it in my life and how much free time I would get back to work or do something else more constructive. I lasted about thirty-six hours. I went back to it because I missed my mindless time. When I play, I can be "off" and not think. I need that break. We all do. All I ask is for you to be mindful and not use that mindless activity to avoid life. If you need that break and need to be mindless, find *your* way. Watch a TV show, read a magazine, take a nap. Frivolous is okay. Self-love is giving yourself a break. Give yourself a time limit so you are not avoiding life and feelings completely, and when you are refreshed, move on to the next thing you need to do for you. Being self-nurturing is also self-love. You are always with yourself; you cannot leave yourself, so you may as well love yourself.

There is no outside love that will be greater than the one you can find for yourself, within yourself. When you open your heart, what you have inside can emerge. Each of us carries pieces of wisdom, and it is up to you to share all of these truths. They are needed by everyone as well as yourself. This is the greatest gift you can give to yourself or another. Love has the ability to transcend all the years of pain and suffering. The power of love is the reason that love is part of the Spiral of Healing. Love the beauty that lies within. Trust your heart, know your soul, believe in yourself. Love is the connection between the heart, mind, and soul, and his includes all types of love: love of self, romantic love, friendship love, love for your pets, love for nature, and love for the Earth. Love is held by and in the light.

Show self-compassion, show self-love.
This wisdom of the all is great but no one knows them-selves better than you.
Do not be afraid to enter the house unknown.
The house unknown holds all the gifts.

Self-love is your greatest gift for true manifestation in your life. You must be in a place of great self-love to bring desired change and outcome into your life. When you allow yourself the freedom to venture into the unknown parts of self for healing, it is there that you will find your greatest gifts.

Journal Prompts

- Take a few breaths. Imagine that you can see your heart. Tap into your heart. What do you see there? What do you feel there? How will you tend to it?

- Imagine you will tend to it as you would a garden, and allow it to bloom and grow in the light of all that is. What would shift for you?

- Think about being in your open and loving heart. Ask yourself, *How will my life transform when I step into this heart space?*

PART 3

HOW TO SHOW UP

CHAPTER 12

Meditation

M editation is the practice of focusing your attention to help you feel calm and give you a clearer awareness about your life. Eastern philosophies have recognized the health benefits of meditation for thousands of years. Meditation is now widely practiced in the West, with the belief that it has positive effects on health.

I came to know meditation when I was learning to become a hypnotherapist. The first twenty-five hours of the training involved learning about creative visualization and guided meditations. In hypnosis, you go into an altered state of consciousness in order to access the subconscious mind. What I learned is that the altered state accessed during hypnosis is the same altered state one is in during meditation. In essence, meditation is an altered state of consciousness; when we meditate, we enter a state of consciousness different from the one we're in while we're, say, cooking dinner or driving down the highway. It's a state that is alert and aware in a different way from the one you are in as you're reading this sentence.

The meditation I practiced when I first started (and honestly, for many years thereafter) was guided by myself or someone else. I eventually began to meditate without outside guidance, quietly guiding myself where I wanted to go. In the last two years, I have fully embraced silent meditation and allow myself to be present in the silence and on my breath while I allow for whatever needs to show up for me to do so. In short, we all do what works best for us. I do not believe there is a right or wrong way to meditate.

If you were to do a Google search on meditation, you would find many strong opinions about the way it must be practiced in order to be effective. HealthandYoga.com states, "These days, meditation is commonly understood to mean some form of spiritual practice where one sits down with eyes closed and empties the mind to attain inner peace, relaxation, or even an experience of God." I think that sort of statement is the reason so many find the idea of meditating intimidating and why the belief is out there that there is a right way to meditate. I am not asking those who believe that to change their beliefs; I am simply offering another perspective, one that does not judge one way of meditation as better or more effective than another but acknowledges that all ways are valuable and that each person will find their own right way, the way that works best for them.

There are many misnomers about meditation that I

hear from friends and clients. The commonly held limiting beliefs I hear include:

- I can't do it.
- Every time I try it is too hard.
- I fall asleep.
- My thoughts get in the way.
- I can't relax.
- It takes too much time.
- I can only do it a certain way.
- There is a right way to do it.

Hopefully, by the end of this chapter you will see that these beliefs really are not reasons to prevent you from meditating in your daily life. When I am asked, "How do I start?" my simple answer is, "You start by starting." Seriously. That said, I also know that meditation is something you need to learn to do, and the way you learn to do it is by practicing.

By making the choice to heal, grow, and become, you have empowered yourself to arrive wherever you want to ultimately arrive. The most direct pathway to reaching those goals and that healing is meditation. Meditation allows you to find the answers that are already within you. Your soul's wisdom is waiting to be tapped into; are you ready to listen? When we quiet our mind, we tune into our body and can get into our heart space. It is important to tune into our bodies because we are energetic beings. As such, every experience we have ever had is stored in our cellular memory, and we must heal at the part of the body that is holding on to pain.

Meditation is a key and vital element in personal growth. Light is the way to love, to all the knowing which resides inside of you. Do not turn your back on light. The wisdom is unfolding before you. Allow the words to enter and take shape. The lesson is of peace. This is what is needed. Peace, love, acceptance, joy. Use your heart to lead the way. You will not be led astray. There is much to be learned by connecting to your soul's knowledge. Open your heart and let it flow to you, lift up into the light, and float in the love and knowing of the soul. At a soul level, we are all at peace. We have complete knowing and trust within the self because there is no comparison to the other. At the soul level is acceptance of the essence that is; there is no right or wrong, there just is. Imagine pure isness, being, acceptance, embracing of the one who you are.

We all came to this incarnation knowing this love, peace, acceptance, isness, stillness, self-love, and be-ingness, but then we lost it. One can see it again when it is safe to touch it again. Some come back into the expanded, trans-cended state; some do not. Either way, it is okay, because all have a certain journey and purpose in this lifetime, and therefore, all journeys are needed.

The sacred journey of the soul happens in the breath. It allows for us to connect to our deepest self and to our de-

sire to manifest. It is like a sacred dance, the same but changing. The breath comes in and out, but each breath has an opportunity to bring something new.

Nothing happens in a bubble. We are all connected to the flow of the formless. It is up to us, through meditation, to enter the flow of the formless and allow form to manifest. Form is that which we *can* touch: the objects and people in your life, the building you live in, the work that you do. The formless is made up of your ideas, inspirations, and intentions. It is made up of the energy around you that all have the ability to tap into through trust in one's self and allowing one's self to go to the places of wisdom inside where all internal knowing is stored.

You are the one who is able to traverse time and space. Inner reflection and clarity are available to you as you prepare yourself for the answers to the questions you ask as you enter meditation. Be patient with yourself; it is okay not to know. Sometimes, we must sit in the not knowing until it is time for us to know. We must be patient and sit with the uncertainty, trusting that the knowing will come when we are ready to hear the answers. The trick is being able to live with the not knowing, yet able to flow through the unknown with confidence and grace as we hold onto trust of self and trust in the universe that we will be guided to the exact right destination.

Each moment is a state of being. In each moment, we are being called to accept the isness of each moment. Focusing on your breath in meditation brings you into the present moment. The destination, that moment, will be the being state for you until you are ready to travel again. As long as you travel with trust in your heart for yourself, you cannot land in the wrong space.

The trust must be placed inward, not on the expectation that someone or something outside of yourself will have to change in order for you to change. We have no control to change another. Hoping someone else will change or that a situation will change only robs us of our own internal knowing. It indicates that we are wishing for something outside of us to change in order for us to feel better internally. If something or someone outside of us happens to change and we feel better because of that, but have not shifted internally, that state of feeling better will only be temporary.

It is through meditation that you find your voice and connect with yourself. It is in the space between our thoughts where we access the voice of our soul. This is the space wherein we hear the messages that are ours. In fact, these messages have always been there, but most of us do not sit long enough to hear them. When you sit and quiet your mind, you are able to hear the messages, the knowing of your soul.

We are one, and therefore, the messages are universal. They are there for the rising of the vibration for all. They are like a roadmap of light that allows us to enter into the knowing. This is the gift you receive when you set aside time for you and begin to meditate.

My hope for you is that you allow the wisdom and words to flow through you. Meditation brings inner peace and harmony, a sense of calm and ease. It is being in the flow of the energy and allowing the energy to transport you to a deep place within your soul, the part of you that knows "I am whole; I am no longer seeking outside of myself to find out who I am and how I am to be." Instead, you trust the wisdom that rises and finds expression in words of truth. This is the language of your soul; that is the inner connectedness of your heart and soul. That is the part that is open to simultaneously listen and speak through you. That is the voice that you can hear from within, the one that is here to remind you, "I am enough."

Let's begin with those annoying thoughts that pop into your head the minute you close your eyes to meditate. I know what happens because it still happens to me, even after all these years. This is normal. The idea that is important to accept is that your thoughts are going to come. Remember, you are not your thoughts. The minute you close your eyes, whether you are doing a guided or a silent meditation, all of a sudden all of the thoughts will come in. Sometimes you may hear this referred to as "monkey mind." In other words, your thoughts are jumping all over the place. Thoughts about your to-do list, such as "I have to pick up bananas," "I have to make a doctor's appointment," "I have to call my mother, father, friend..." "I have to post something on Facebook," "I have to pick up my child at 3:00..." If we fight those thoughts and get angry about them interrupting us, they will only come back stronger. They *want* to distract you and get in your way because you have given so much importance to them. They carry a lot of weight in your daily life. We are afraid we are going to forget them, and in order not to forget them, we need to be reminded over and over again. They will therefore keep pushing at you until they are acknowledged.

I have a trick to offer you to deal with those pesky thoughts: acknowledge and thank them as they show up. When we acknowledge the thoughts and thank them for showing up, we are letting them know that we will remember them later. When those random thoughts appear for me, I imagine holding my hand up, palm facing out, telling the thought, "I got it, you can move on now." Once that is done, I can then come back to my breath or listen to the one guiding the meditation. You are able to do this too. As you begin to meditate, as the thoughts enter your awareness, just thank them and bring your focus back to the present moment, which is your breath and your meditation. Thank as many thoughts as there are come, as often as they come. As you get practiced and meditate more and more often, those thoughts will enter with less and less frequency. You will find that you will be able to more easily move them off and away so you can come back to you.

A person may consider meditation as worship or prayer. But meditation is simply awareness. Any time you do something with awareness, it's meditation. Washing the dishes while you gaze out the window is meditation, showering is meditation, walking and being present during the walk is meditation. Consider the things you spend time doing each day. Which are meditative for you?

It is well known that meditation offers psychological, physical, emotional and spiritual benefits. In fact, I recommend to all of my clients that they find a way to incorporate some form of meditation into their life. It can be for five minutes a day. It can be consciously focusing on your breath every time you get stuck at a red light. The point is to start somewhere in order to reap the positive benefits.

Meditation does not have to be a spiritual experience for you, but the spiritual dimension of your life can absolutely blossom through meditation. Experienced meditators often describe feeling a blissful wholeness and a deep inner connection to all of life. They feel incredible depths of inner peace—a peace that is beyond all understanding and description—one that lies within us all, and meditation is the key to awakening this unfathomable dimension of freedom.

Meditation is a mind/body connection, and therefore, the mind and body must learn to work together. If you need to start with just one minute of practice, that is where you start. You then do two minutes, then three, until you are able to meditate for longer and longer periods of time. Eventually you will find the way that works best for you. What works for me may not work for you. Some people like listening to music, while others want to hear the sounds of the ocean. Others prefer silent meditation, while some may want a mantra to focus on or to be guided. Some may need to sit cross legged on the floor, some may need to recline or lie down. How you practice is a judgement-free zone as far as I am concerned. What is important is not *how* you meditate but that you are finding the time *to* meditate. When you make that time, that is self-care. That is you telling yourself that you are important, you are worthy, you matter, and this is why it's such a critical component of self-care and healing.

In hypnosis, one of the foundational principles of the deeper mind is that the harder you try to do something, the less chance you have of doing it. This is called the Law of Reverse Effect. "Try" is actually a failure word to the deeper mind. When the subconscious mind hears the word "try," it interprets it as "do not" or "cannot." If you are trying to do something the subconscious knows this because it hears the words you are saying either aloud or to yourself. The deeper mind will work against your trying efforts. This is because the imagination will win over the intellect. For example, if I tell you, "Try not to think about a pink dog," what happens? You can't help but to think of a pink dog.

When I work with my clients, this is one of the first things I teach. I ask them to remove the word "try" from their conversations. If I catch them using it in sessions, I have them replace it with another more positive word of intention. I ask them to become mindful of it, to catch themselves and self-correct in their daily conversations. Do we really want to *try* to take a walk? If I *tried* to take a walk, but never put my sneakers on, I did not take a walk, nor did I really make an effort to do so. Either do something or don't do something. Work toward a goal, make progress on a project, go for a walk, take time to meditate, set an intention to complete a task, make that phone call. Use positive words with intention. Words have energy, and as we express our self, we are in the vibration of the word we choose. Because "try" is a failure word, get out of that vibration and into the vibration of a positive, intentional, action word. You can *do* anything.

We have the wisdom within. We must sit. We must quiet the mind. We must listen to the inner knowing and wisdoms that we already carry inside. These wisdoms were born with us. We simply never learned how to access them. Meditation allows you to peer through a looking glass into your soul. When you meditate, you create the space to look inside and learn what needs attention. When you meditate, you move the thinking mind out of the way and allow the wisdom you were born with to rise up into your awareness in order that you may access it. That wisdom will give you the words you need. It will show you what you need to see, when you need to see it. Sometimes, the insights may not make sense right away. Sometimes, you might question, "Is this even real?" I am asking you to trust yourself, to allow, to be, and to observe. Your truth will flow through you when you are truly ready to allow it. You will know you are *not* ready when your reaction is to dismiss the wisdom and knowledge that comes to you. You will not trust it and will disregard it as untruth,

234 • JANET PHILBIN

perhaps because it is a truth you are not yet ready to "see." Be an explorer of your own self. As you meditate, you allow your truth to emerge. Even if it is not what you expect, I invite you to allow for it.

If you are in a place in your life where you are looking to make choices and get clarification, validation, or guidance, and are looking outside of yourself to do so, you are not looking in the right place. The best decisions for you will not come from what you hear from others but from what you hear from yourself. Meditation allows you to listen to your self, and it is important to trust yourself in all ways. To know from deep within that the path you are on is the right one for you. We all have a choice to move forward into accepting your own healing.

Journal Prompts

- Take a few minutes to write down your past experiences with meditation.

- Write down what about it was challenging and what was easy.

- What limiting beliefs (if any) do you have about meditation?

- When you are able to easily enter into meditation, what goals do you have for yourself?

- How do you imagine that meditation will help you on a day-to-day basis?

CHAPTER 13

Write in the Damn Journal Already

In the mid 1990s I read *Simple Abundance* by Sarah Ban Breathnach. The book was one of Oprah's early book club picks and, therefore, all the rage. I may have found it through Oprah, or a friend may have told me about it because of Oprah, but either way I found myself going to the bookstore (there was no Amazon back then) to purchase it. If you have never heard about this book, the subtitle is *A Daybook of Comfort and Joy*, and it is most certainly that, if you allow yourself to follow its guidance.

The book begins in January, and each day provides you with a passage. I loved it because it was simple, and the readings were short and quick. As you read through January, the author describes on each day a different principle and gives the reader a different project to complete. Some of these projects are craft-style projects, so now is a great time to present the disclaimer that I do not do crafts. In fact, I consider myself an anti-crafter, so much so that, as the leader of my daughter's Girl Scouts troop for twelve years, the only crafts we did were the ones that were mandatory in order to earn badges. If we could avoid a craft by doing another activity, even if it meant more work for me, that is what we did.

The project for January that was most valuable to me at the time, and that I committed to doing, was creating a gratitude journal. Remember, this was 1996, and gratitude was not a "thing" the way it is today. Sarah's only requirement was to write a list at the end of each day of five things you were grateful for in your life on that day. I liked the idea that I did not have to write a *Dear Diary* type entry; I only had to write a simple list.

I want to give you some context so you can understand more completely that time in my life. My husband and I were in the middle of the crisis of infertility. We were engrossed in all of the medical treatments available at the time, and to say it was stressful would be an understatement. I was working full time as a social worker in long-term care, and I was depressed. This book became a lifeline for me, and my gratitude journal became a mental health saver. It was as if someone threw me a life preserver so I would not drown in the deep end of the pool, enabling me to swim to the side.

Infertility is undeniably experienced as a crisis. You feel out of control, as the thing you want most in your life seems totally out of reach. You have no idea if you will ever become pregnant or give birth to a baby. I began writing in my gratitude journal nightly, and each day I read the entry that was there for me in *Simple Abundance*. Some days, I felt so badly that all I was able to write in my journal was:

I'm breathing
I'm breathing
I'm breathing
I'm breathing
I'm breathing.

That is how my life went for more than four years. When I finally did become pregnant, I did not stop journaling my gratitude. I was committed by that point and wanted to stay emotionally healthy through the pregnancy. Pregnancy after infertility is not easy. You are not naive; you know what can still go wrong. The most important thing I did for myself was keep up this practice. What I didn't know was that it would help me to an even greater degree in the future.

I was someone who, after giving birth, experienced postpartum depression. I would say it started about two weeks after my daughter was born. Luckily, I did not have a severe case or one that lasted for months. However, the way my experience presented was, every day at 5pm, I felt as if a dark cloud were descending upon me. When this darkness came, I could not function. I could not be with the baby. I needed someone to be there to take her from me until the cloud lifted, which was usually about two hours later.

This feeling shocked me. After more than four years battling infertility and then experiencing a pregnancy with complications (as well as a complicated delivery), I assumed I would be happy. And I was. I was in love with that baby and only wanted to be with her. So, when this darkness descended, I knew it was hormonal. One day, when my husband was at home at 5pm, I felt the darkness coming, handed him the baby, and told him I needed to take a walk. It was mid to late February in New York, and it was freezing out, but that didn't matter. As I walked up the block, I noticed the small tree branch right at my eye level. On the branch, just where two branches met, making a V shape, was a droplet of water, just sitting there. I stopped and looked at that drop of water. I saw how beautiful it was, being held by the tree, looking both gentle and beautiful as it reflected the sinking sunlight's rays. The first thought I had after taking in all the details of this drop of water was one of gratitude for the moment. For seeing this drop. I decided it would be one of the things for which I'd write I was grateful in my journal that night.

That moment began to bring me out of the PPD. It began to bring me back to myself. It reminded me that I still had things to be grateful for. This was before I'd begun exploring the concept of spirituality, before I knew that connecting with nature was a way to bring one back to the present moment. But it did anyway. It moved me. It shifted me. Because I was already journaling, because I'd made it a daily practice, I was able to access it easily without working on it, without having to figure it out. It was just there. This story illustrates why it is important to have such a practice. A practice becomes part of you, and you can fall back on it and access it when necessary.

I find that there is such resistance to journaling. I know that my clients are sincere in their desire to cope more effectively and heal, yet they often resist my encouragement and direction to journal between sessions. That leads me to ask, "Why is this? Why is it that people come to me week after week for psychotherapy, hypnotherapy, and healing yet are so resistant to picking up a pen and putting it to paper?"

One way I understand this resistance is that avoiding journaling is another way of avoiding feelings. It is a way to stay in denial and avoid emotional pain. It presents such a dichotomy, because avoiding pain actually causes more of it. When we get it out on paper, it is out. As though you were slowly opening a bottle of carbonated soda, the bubbles release in a way such that the fizz does not explode all over the place. You are letting it out in a way that is "safer," so to speak.

In order to journal, you must write. In order to write, you must tap into your inner landscape—your feelings, experiences, thoughts, responses, and beliefs. That requires making time for you and allowing your inner voice to actually *have* a voice. It is a time for you to stop being with the business of whatever is taking you away from hearing your inner voice. Picking up the pen and putting it to paper is like holding on to that bottle top, deciding to open it slowly and carefully. When you put the feelings, thoughts, beliefs, fears, and hang-ups on paper, you are giving them a chance to be heard. You are getting them out of your head and beginning to diffuse both them and their toxicity. As you write, you are giving that part of the inner you that has been hiding, maybe even the one who was hiding in the closet, a safe place to express himself or herself.

When I ask my clients to journal, I do not tell them to immediately go out and buy a beautiful journal. I do own those kinds of journals myself, and the times when I've bought them occurred because, for some reason, I was drawn to a particular journal. However, you do not have to have a beautiful or expensive journal.

I do have one rule, however, and that is if you do buy a journal, it needs to have pages that are blank. There can be no pre-printed lines. I encourage my clients to use blank computer paper if they are leaning toward the excuse that they need to go out and buy a journal before they can begin to journal. The reason for this is that when you journal, I want you to have the freedom to allow your thoughts, feelings, dreams, and pain to arrive on the page any way they want. I do not want you to pay attention to grammar, spelling, punctuation, or neatness. Maybe you'll want to write with your eyes closed or while you are walking. Your writing does not need form. It simply needs to be given the freedom to be put on the page. A blank page allows you to be in the flow of it as you write.

Even if you don't know what to write, simply start writing. You can even start with "I don't know what to write" or "I hate Janet. Why is she making me write this? I am so angry." If necessary, keep writing those sentences until something else comes. Something else *will* come; you just have to allow yourself the time and space to sit in the discomfort of writing.

People want to know how long it will take for something to come when they do not feel like writing in their journals and are beginning with the above or similar sentences. In my own personal experience, it does not take more than five minutes or so for those "stuck" thoughts to get out of the way and for you to be able to access what really needs to be given a voice.

Journaling is an expression of self. It is a creative way to express your thoughts and feelings. It involves the throat chakra. If you are having trouble journaling, tune your awareness into your throat chakra, close your eyes, and take a breath. Give yourself a moment to see what it feels like, and then do one of the journal prompts in this book to access what is happening in your throat that is blocking you from writing in your journal.

One of the primary purposes of a journal is to get the story in your head out on paper. Once it is out, you can look at it, explore it, deconstruct it, begin to understand why it began in the first place, and ask yourself questions about why you continue to hold onto it. Plus, when you get it out of your head and onto paper, you are also getting it out of your body.

Oh, and guess what? You do not have to keep what you write. Another excuse I hear frequently is that clients don't want to journal because they fear it will be found and read by someone else. Or, they never want to have to look at it again. Those are really poor reasons for not journaling. I have never read or been taught in any of the many, many courses I have taken over the last thirty years as a clinician that one of the requirements of journaling is keeping the journal. If you don't want to keep it, I am giving you permission, right now, to burn it. Burn your journal pages, and burn them with intention. Put them in a fireplace, a firepit, a coffee can, or anywhere that's safe to burn things. As you watch those pages burn, as the words on them are released in the universe, set an intention that those aspects of yourself receive a healing. Letting go and releasing in this way allows you to be open and ready to heal. This is a very powerful process.

Journal Prompts

- Take a pause here and allow yourself to write the words in your heart right now. What came up for you about journaling as you read this chapter?

- Write anything at all. Let the words flow out of you, and write until there are no more words.

- Pay attention to how you feel when you are finished writing.

- Do you feel lighter, better, not as scared, willing to journal again?

CHAPTER 14

Hypnosis and Hypnotherapy

I specialize in inner-child healing. Hypnosis is a powerful method of healing that is extremely effective in helping one heal from emotional trauma as well as childhood trauma. It is also very effective for anxiety, depression, and coping with daily life stressors.

I use hypnotherapy with my clients with the goal of inner child healing. The method I practice allows one to look at current upsets and past memories from a safe space. In this safe space, one is able to move through the feelings that come up and emerge on the other side of them. The end result is a much stronger ability to accept the "as is" of the present moment.

If you look up the word hypnosis, you will find a variety of definitions for it. While they will vary slightly, the common theme is that hypnosis, like meditation, is an altered state of consciousness. During this altered state of consciousness, we can make shifts, and as a result of these shifts, changes can occur in day-to-day life. I know that description is not terribly clear, but because I've offered you "official" definitions of various terms throughout this book, I'm doing the same here in the spirit of consistency.

A.M. Krasner, Ph.D., author of *The Wizard Within*, defines hypnosis as "a process which produces relaxation, distraction of the conscious mind, heightened suggestibility, and increased awareness, allowing access to the subconscious mind through the imagination. It also produces the ability to experience thoughts and images as real." The reason it produces the ability to experience thoughts and images as real is that the deeper mind, the subconscious, cannot differentiate between reality and imagination. Krasner goes on to say, "For the process to be effective, there are two components that must be present: belief and expectation." In other words, for someone to be able to be hypnotized, they have to have the belief that they can *be* hypnotized and the expectation that hypnosis *will* work for them. In my work, if I am challenged to hypnotize someone, I will not, because I know that I am not stronger than someone else's mind.

We are each in charge of our own minds and thoughts, so if someone challenges me to hypnotize them, saying, "You can't hypnotize me," and I try anyway, it won't work because they are holding firm the belief that they can't be hypnotized as well as the expectation that it won't work. If I were to attempt anyway, I would be coming from ego—Western psychology's ego—believing I have more power over that person than they have over themselves.

There is no room for ego in this work. I view the work that I do as sacred, and I approach it with humility. Each client who chooses to work with me is coming to me for help with their pain and suffering, and it is my honor to be a helper in their process of healing.

All we have ever experienced or learned in our life is stored in our subconscious mind, and we have the ability to access all of our memories from an altered state of consciousness. Hypnosis allows the conscious mind to move out of the way in order to gain access into the deeper—or subconscious—mind.

It is my intention to demystify hypnosis for you. When you are in hypnosis, you are merely getting into a state of deep relaxation, where the thinking mind (left side of the brain) is occupied so that we can open the door and enter the right side of the brain--the creative side. We do not want reasoning or intellect to get in the way. In order to do this, we give the left brain something to think about, such as a beautiful beach, a mountain, counting up or down, or focusing on relaxing a body part. In my practice, in order to help my clients achieve a hypnotic state, I use a lot of chakra-balancing imagery. This not only occupies the mind but it relaxes the body and balances the chakras at the same time.

In order to understand the subconscious mind better, I encourage you to think about a computer. Just like a computer can store endless amounts of information, the subconscious stores all of your life experiences. If you add new data on your computer, it gets saved onto the hard drive. Once there, in order to edit the data, you must go into that file to make the changes. That is how the deeper mind works. All of our life experiences are recorded into the hard drive of the deeper mind, and we access those memories through different prompts. When we access them, it is as if we are choosing a file to open. Through that file, we are able to get in touch with specific memories and experiences. According to Krasner, "The computer-like subconscious mind can be programmed, or reprogrammed, to change habits and attitudes...to change your life." (p.80.)

In my practice of clinical hypnosis, the goal is always to help my clients achieve a specific level of healing. Sometimes, I'm asked if I can help people with smoking cessation or weight loss, and my answer is, "Only if you want to get to the root of the reason why you began to smoke or over-eat." I do not believe in quick fixes or putting a Band-Aid on a gushing wound. If a client wants to dig in, uncover, and understand himself, I am open to help. If, however, he wants strong post hypnotic suggestions to end a behavior without that deeper healing, they need to find a hypnotist who will do that. Along those lines, I will also not have someone return to a painful memory only to find the memory and then leave it there, out in the open, without going through a healing process. Healing the injured part or the injured inner child is *always* the goal. When I take a client back in time through hypnosis, the process is always safe, and the client is always in control.

Here are some points commonly held within the field of hypnosis that will help you understand how hypnosis works within the deeper mind and why it is so effective in helping someone heal.

- In the altered state, suggestions are acted upon much more powerfully.
- Hypnosis allows people to use more of their own potential.
- The shift in consciousness allows us to tap into our natural abilities and learn more quickly.
- Hypnosis creates a heightened state of awareness, allowing us to make changes more quickly.
- Hypnosis creates a state of concentrated attention, therefore the focus of your attention is narrower allowing for a higher level of awareness on a focal point.
- Suggestions are more likely to be accepted by the subconscious mind.
- Hypnosis is a safe and natural state that allows us to examine the roots of problems and offer alternative solutions.
- Hypnosis allows access to parts of your mind that are usually out of reach to your consciousness.
- We learn either through repetition or one very powerful event.
- When we receive communication, it is at every level of consciousness, which is why working with hypnosis and the chakras at the same time is so effective.

- Metaphors are the language of the deeper mind. When we can relate things together through the use of a metaphor, it makes the concept believable and/or doable. For example, imagine that you are as light as a feather, and as a feather, you can float and drift. We all have seen feathers floating in a breeze and therefore know this is true. Since we know it can be true, we can also imagine it happening.

- The deeper mind cannot tell real from imaginary.

- The deeper mind has no sense of time. For example, have you ever been driving, and once you got to the destination, you didn't recall the drive? Or, while reading a great book, you lost all sense of time? These are just two examples of being in an altered or trance-like state. In hypnosis, we are going into that trance-like state on purpose.

- The deeper mind takes everything literally, which is why post-hypnotic suggestions are powerful and important when putting new coping skills in place.

There are many myths floating around when it comes to hypnosis. When I share that I am a hypnotherapist, I am almost always asked two questions: "Do you use a pendulum to hypnotize someone?" and "Will you make me quack like a duck?" The answer to both is no. (Yes, I actually own two pendulums, but they are not used to put someone into hypnosis, and I have never made someone quack like a duck.)

Hypnosis is sacred work. The deeper mind is not a playground within which to have fun with someone for the sake of proving how powerful and skilled I am. As stated previously, that approach would be coming from ego, and there is no room for ego in healing and hypnosis.

Myths Surrounding Hypnosis

People will surrender their will, become powerless and lose self-control under hypnosis

This is simply not true. Your awareness is heightened under hypnosis, and when hypnotized, you are in control of yourself. In the story I shared at the beginning of the book of being hypnotized on stage, when I was trying to get the shitting bird off of my finger and then kissed the guy at the bar, all of those events happened because I agreed to them. The hypnotist could not *make* me do them. That is why he tested people for the show--to see who was willing to be open to taking his suggestions. I was in control in that situation, and if I wanted to come out of hypnosis, I could have.

In 2008 I had a client who came to me for inner child healing. This woman was born with a birth defect, and by the time I met her, when she was in her mid-thirties, she had undergone thirty-five surgeries, the first having oc- curred within twenty-four hours of her birth. When we began doing hypnosis, I brought in the image of a bright white healing light. When I introduced this image, she bolted upright on my couch and had to stop the hypnosis session, which she could of course do because she was in control. What neither of us realized going into the session was that imagery of white light was a significant trigger for her. When I brought in the light, she immediately felt as if she were on a gurney in the operating room, with the big operating room light shining down on her as it had so many times when she was a young child. Through hypnotherapy, we were eventually able to heal that trigger, and successfully used the white light imagery moving forward. I share this case with you to illustrate that, even under hypnosis, the client is always in control. The hypnotist is never more in control of your mind than you are.

People will share their secrets under hypnosis

Under hypnosis you will not share anything that you do not want to share. When I ask my clients to go back in time to the origin of a big feeling, they are choosing to which time and to which event in their life to return. If, under hypnosis, they recall something they do not want to share, they do not have to share it. I know this to be true because I have experienced it myself in my own work under hypnosis. The Svengali Effect proposes the assumption that a person under hypnosis can be made to do something against his/her will. The truth, however, is that in stage or clinical hypnosis, people only follow the hypnotic suggestions they are ethically and morally comfortable with and will not do things that go against their basic fundamental beliefs.

In hypnosis, the hypnotist has more power over the client's mind

I have no power over my clients. I cannot gain control over my clients. Clients are able to be hypnotized if they want to be, not because I am controlling them to be in hypnosis but because being hypnotized is their choice. As I have stated, no one has more control over you and your mind than you do.

Under hypnosis, the client can be put to sleep

You are not asleep while in hypnosis. You are in a deep, altered state of consciousness. Now, have clients *fallen* asleep while working with me in meditation? Yes, they have. I can tell when this happens--they snore, their breathing changes, and they stop responding to my questions. At this point, I have to bring them out of their sleep and back into connection to me and the meditation. However, in hypnosis, you can go so deeply into an altered state that while it can feel like you're sleeping, you aren't. You can always tell that you are not clinically asleep because when you are counted back into consciousness, you are aware and alert by the end of the counting process. If you were asleep, you would not "wake up" when you were counted up. You will also remember all that occurred during the hypnosis session.

Only weak-willed or weak-minded people can be hypnotized

The reality is quite the opposite. If you are able to be hypnotized, it proves that you are very strong-minded. Remember, it is one's choice to be under hypnosis.

Some people will lose consciousness in hypnosis

This is false. The practice of clinical hypnosis has to be administered carefully. The client must be emotionally ready, as the healing can be quite powerful and profound. Because there is an inward focus of attention, some external happenings (like a car horn beeping) may not be noticed. The majority of people will remember everything that happens in hypnosis. The only danger of hypnosis—as is the case with any therapeutic practice—occurs if the person conducting the hypnosis is not properly trained. You want to be sure before you enter into hypnosis with a therapist that they have the proper training, skills, and experience for your needs and goals.

When a client is working with me, hypnosis is conducted in a very careful way. I follow a model of treatment that allows for safe healing. As I explained in the Heal section of chapter 11 via the onion metaphor, there are many layers to healing, so there really is no way to predict or guarantee how many sessions someone may need to reach their healing goals. Everyone is unique; there is no one-size-fits-all. When working with me, your treatment and care is tailored to you. That said, there are five basic stages in a hypnosis session.

Induction

During induction, the client is guided into a hypnotic state, which can be achieved through a variety of techniques. I most commonly use guided meditation to bring a client into an altered state of consciousness, the hypnotic state.

Deepening

During deepening, the client moves even further away from the conscious mind and goes into a more detached state of awareness. From this deep, altered state we can access the subconscious mind and begin to uncover the aspects of self that are in need of a healing.

Uncovering/healing work

This phase of the session is when I take the client back in time to the part of them, their inner child, that is in pain and holding onto the feelings that are affecting them in the present. Once we find this memory, I work with the client to gain perspective and understanding of what was happening at that time. The client is now in a dissociative state, not reliving the event (revivification) but instead observing the event from a safe distance. It is during this time that I have the client tune into their chakras and understand how and where the event has been affecting them physically. Once we have all the details and a good understanding of what needs to be healed, I take the client through the transformational healing process I have been trained in by William Bezmen, Ph.D., at Pathways to

Health. This process heals the emotional wounds at a cellular level; allows for the release of the pain from the time; and makes emotional, energetic, and physical space to put healing in place.

Post-Hypnotic Suggestions

A post hypnotic suggestion is a suggestion made while a client is still in the altered state. This suggestion is given to the deeper mind and put in place of the old, faulty belief systems that were just removed. The client, under hypnosis, understands and sees how these new coping skills will be used in their day-to-day life moving forward and how the issue they were struggling with is transformed. This is the final part of the healing process.

De-Hypnotization

This is the final stage of hypnosis, when the client is brought back to the present, usually through counting up from one to five. Once dehypnotized, the client is awake, alert, and feeling really good about and proud of themselves.

Each of us, when taking on something new, does research. If you want to find a new doctor, hire a new accountant, or apply to college or a new job, what is the first thing you do? You probably utilize Google, and part of what you're interested in finding is what others have to say about a particular practitioner. You want to learn what someone else's experience has been in order to better assess whether this person or place is a good fit for you. You are asking yourself, "Can this person help me with the areas in my life where I am struggling?" When you approach working with a hypnotherapist, you should do the same careful research.

I want to give you some guidance here so that when you explore this for yourself, you will have a way to understand what to expect. Please understand that what I am sharing is based on the way that *I* work; all therapists and hypnotherapists work differently. Therefore, finding the right fit for you is important. I fully acknowledge and embrace that I am not the right fit for everyone. If you are not ready to do the deep work, find someone with whom you can graze the surface. When you are ready, find someone who can take you deeper into your healing, if you'd like. You may have to test out a few people before you find the helper who is a fit for your needs and personality.

When a client comes to work with me, I let them know certain things about how I work and what they can expect.

This is what I share:

You will not be cured in one session

A complete healing in one session happens very infrequently. In fact, in the seventeen years I have been practicing hypnotherapy, it has happened exactly one time. This is not a reflection on how skilled a practitioner is; it is a reflection of the fact that healing happens in layers. In the one case where one of my clients healed in one session, it was because the person knew the incident from their childhood, which was a near drowning, and the memory of it was triggered in the present while pregnant. She had a major panic attack. The near drowning was never a forgotten memory. When she had a panic attack during her pregnancy, she felt like (and believed) she could not breathe because the baby was sitting on her rib cage, and she felt as though her lungs were compressed, which is exactly what happened when she was a young child. We had a direct link to a known past event that was significantly impacting her in the present. She was willing to go back to that event and heal her inner-child trauma from the day she almost drowned. Her panic attacks stopped immediately, and she never needed me for a follow-up session (though she knows I am still available to her if anything else shows up).

I never specify exactly how many sessions healing will take

Because of the onion, I never know what is going to come up. My clients may think they know what will come up, but neither of us knows for sure. I had a client I'll refer to as Crystal, who was struggling with infertility. We had done many sessions of hypnosis to heal the emotional wounds of her inner child, which were impacting her emotionally. These old emotional wounds were affecting her in the present in her ability to cope with infertility. One of her recurrent themes was that she was not seen as important by her family. Finally, during one session, we came to a memory of her as a young child of seven or eight years old. Crystal recalled coming into the house with her sand pail and being excited to show her dad her beach "finds." She was ignored, unable to share what she found, and told to let the adults talk, not to bother them right now. This was the moment Crystal internalized all of these feelings of lack, of not feeling good enough or important enough. These significant beliefs of not feeling important and being ignored became part of her belief system and began to shape the way she thought about herself in the world and within her family.

This healing was a turning point for her emotional growth. Crystal had not previously recalled this day. There was no way to anticipate that a seemingly benign event would have such long-lasting emotional effects. This is why I cannot predict the length of time or how many sessions it will take to heal. I ask for people to plan for a minimum of six sessions, but the length of time it will take to heal also depends on the level of work you are willing to do. How committed are you? Will you participate in weekly appointments? Are you going to meditate and journal in between sessions?

The chances of getting all of one's past out in one session is very low. However, to experience a transformational healing in six or ten sessions, levels and layers of healing will happen.

The other mitigating factor when it comes to how long healing with hypnosis will take is how much work you have done on yourself prior to your first session. If you have never meditated or practiced relaxation techniques before, you will first need to learn how to do that. I will likely need to spend a session or two with you, getting you ready for deeper work. If you are a regular meditator, have worked with other healers, or have done inner child or trauma work before, it will more than likely take fewer sessions to accomplish the level of healing you desire.

I also have to assess the level of trauma being accessed. This isn't like taking an antibiotic, where the doctor can guarantee you that if you take a specific pill for seven days, the infection will be gone. The level of work done is up to you. I am there to support and guide you through it. I am the guide by your side. And I will stay right at your side during your work, but I can only take you to the places you are willing to go.

Finally, how much self-awareness do you have going in? It is up to you to fix you. You have the power and control. It is your decision to heal, just as it is your decision to choose to work with me or not. It is your decision because you and you alone are in charge of your healing.

There is no quick fix

You will have a higher chance of success if you can accept that you are where you are. It doesn't matter where someone else is on their healing journey; you cannot compare yourself to another, as that will only leave you feeling badly and possibly even reinforcing some old belief systems that you are not able to heal or feel better. When you commit to doing deeper work, it creates a space in which to release all expectations and accept where you are on your individual journey. Expectations will only cause you pain. Drop the expectations, and enter the reality of your journey's present moment. When you hold onto expectation, that expectation limits you, because when you do not get what you are expecting and it does not look as you imagined it to look, it becomes "the death of us." After that, we wonder, "Now what? What do I do? This did not work out the way I thought it would." But ask yourself this: What if it works out exactly as it needs to in order for you to reach the next part of your evolution? Had the process gone according to your expected "plan," you would have missed out on some very important learning lessons or gifts. There is no prescription; hypnosis is not a cookie-cutter approach.

CHAPTER 15

Putting It All Together

Do you really believe that the young one inside of you wants to be in pain? I think not. That little one already lived through it and survived. It is up to you to rescue him or her and give that one a safe landing space in your heart. To let him or her embrace being a child again and let the job of adulting be left to the adult you.

Once you are aware of your triggers, your inner child's pain, and your emotions, the next step is to deconstruct it. To deconstruct something usually means to disassemble it, piece by piece. To look at the structure and then take it apart, down to its bare bones, down to its nakedness, so you can see what helped it form. This is where hypnosis can be used to allow healing to happen in a safe and supportive space. When you deconstruct your patterns, your emotional and physical reactions, you need to begin to ask more questions. It is time to go back in time and find the origin of the emotion. To find out the age of the child who first began coping with the strong emotion in the way you, the adult, have continued to cope with it.

As children, we develop coping skills based on our developmental abilities at the time. A child can only cope by using the resources she has available to her. Remember, the deeper mind has no sense of time. We must first assume that our inner child did the best he or she could at that time for their developmental age and with the resources available. This is the truth.

You continue to ask questions. You ask why. You ask how. You ask for descriptions of the situation and the others who were involved. You want to be like a detective, uncovering the clues to find an answer. Consciousness is becoming aware. When I work with clients, I want to take them to a deeper awareness. I want to take that awareness into the physical body and see where that particular emotion/reaction/behavior has taken up residence in the physical body. This is why understanding the chakras is crucial to this work. Noticing how you feel in your body will become your greatest partner in your role as detective.

As I explained earlier, every time we feel a feeling, we feel it *in the body*. It is a feeling because it is something we experience in our being. Ideally, feelings should pass through us in a matter of seconds, but as you now know, that usually does not happen. Instead, we feel a feeling and unconsciously know we don't like the feeling, so we have an immediate reaction to squash the feeling, push it down, hold it, or numb out until it goes away. Or we give

the feeling a name, and it becomes an emotion like anxiety, fear, or depression, at which point we attach a story to
it. Once there is a story attached to it, we get caught up in
that story. Our minds can spin out of control, getting into
all sorts of "what if" scenarios. This robs you of the moment and pulls you into the abyss of worry about the unknown future. The problem here is that the feeling does
not go away. You are either burying it or building stories
and stress around it, and one day it will need to get un-
earthed. Feelings let us know they are there.

Let me bring you back to the deconstruction. We deconstruct by asking lots of questions in the conscious
mind. This can also be done with hypnosis, as the subconscious mind can access the old files, the ones we stored in
the computer of our mind. Once we get to the age, event,
and trauma through the asking of these questions, we can
we can do the transformative inner child healing.

Connecting to yourself and healing your inner child is
important, because if you are not connected to self, you
cannot connect to another. In today's day and age, all of
us spend a lot of time disconnected from the ones right in
front of us. Electronics have disconnected us from the
people who are in the same room! And, it is easy to forget
about others, because when you get lost in the world of
social media you are looking outside of the self, comparing
the self, and really, at that point, you are not connected to
the truth of who you really are. You begin to see yourself
through the lens of how you will appear to others. Because healing is an inside-out process, you must connect

to the self; this is why consciousness is awakening within you. This is your own inner child asking you to connect with them. It is a plea from the deepest part of your heart to be seen, heard, and validated, and to know once and for all that you are enough just as you are.

The inner child must be told the truth. Under hypnosis, you can bring the inner child into a safe place with your loving adult self and tell them the truth about the situation they survived so they can understand it from a higher perspective—from a distance—and gain wisdom.

Through this process, you are guided to reframe the belief system developed about yourself at the time, and you can begin to heal through an undoing of the damage of your limiting thoughts and beliefs about who you thought you were in the world and how you feel about yourself in the world now. You are able to grow in understanding that the situation at that time was just that—at that time. The emotional injuries do not need to continue to have power over your life. You can choose, now that you know the truth, how you are going to show up in the present moment. You re-parent the inner child with compassion and love. You are reframing for the inner child, and empowering the inner child to know they are now safe, seen, and heard. You will give the inner child new wisdom that can now be applied going forward to situations that used to act as a trigger.

When you continue to look outside of yourself, you merely project onto others and perpetuate your story, your belief system about yourself and your life. In essence, you repeat over and over again and get the same results. You are seeking to feel better but instead recreate the same or similar pain. It becomes a self-fulfilling prophecy. But, what if you took that purposeful pause? You are empowered to decide to turn the light toward you, toward the original trauma, toward the injured inner child who needs to be told the truth. You can safely go back there and work with the injured inner child; hear the pain, trauma, and faulty beliefs; and then give that injured one tools to heal. To reconstruct the self from a safe place, from a higher perspective, from a place of wisdom without judgement or limits.

The process of healing includes consciously deconstructing the feeling and getting to the origin of it, whether the source is childhood or culture. Once we are ready to know the wounded one inside, the core pain body can heal that particular aspect of the inner child in pain. This, to me, constitutes complete healing—deconstructing on a conscious level and finding healing on a subconscious level, allowing for freedom and the room necessary for the true self to emerge.

We don't always know on a conscious level how to help the wounded inner child, a deeper way of going inward is through hypnosis. Once we know their pain, we can re-parent as our loving adult self and bring the inner child back into our hearts feeling whole, loved, understood, and forgiven. **That is transformational healing from the depths of our innermost being state.**

As part of the transformational healing process, we can

begin to see the connections between what we did to protect our self as a child and how we use those same coping skills to protect the adult self in the present. When our inner child is in front of us and our old emotions get triggered, the injured inner child is the one both reacting and reenacting. If we do not understand that our reaction now is from something that we developed in the past in order to cope with an event we witnessed or experienced, it will be very hard to make real and lasting change in the present.

A client, whom I will refer to as Emily, had just this experience. As a child, she witnessed horrible physical abuse by her father toward her mother. As a five-year-old girl, she stayed in the room, trying to be invisible, yet at the same time unable to leave because she held the belief that if she was there, the abuse would not be as severe. Now, as an adult, in the face of conflict she wants to be invisible; she does not want to feel. She wants the ugly feelings to just go away.

In her current life, when her pre-teen son got angry, she was not able to handle it or hold the space necessary to allow him his emotions. She wanted his anger to just go away so she could feel better. She had developed a pattern with him of trying to shut his anger down.

During hypnosis, she was able to make the connection and gain an understanding of why she reacted to him in this way. It was a huge *aha* moment when she realized that her reactions to her son were directly connected to her five-year-old self. With this awareness, she became able to be aware of herself and her feelings, and both own them and feel safe within herself, which allows her son the space to be able to express his emotions, even the angry ones.

By being able to hold the space for herself and her son, she is now able to form better connections with him and have a deeper relationship with him, and the depth of the healing is great because what she is really learning is that she can feel safe within herself. She can allow herself to be that conscious parent *and* have a conscious relationship with herself. She can now be in tune with her own emotions and able to take care of the self, who knows who she is as separate from her son. This allows for each of their individual growth as well as a healthy mother/son relationship.

In doing this healing work, Emily was able to move up in the Spiral of Healing through this session and the ones that followed as we continued to work with her younger self and heal at the origin of the emotional pain. This is how we heal—we look back, we help our younger self, we gain a new perspective and share the truth with the one who was in pain all this time. This is freedom; healing allows for emotional freedom.

There is synergy between developing a conscious relationship with yourself and inner-child healing through hypnosis, as we need to re-parent the inner child with the wisdom of consciousness. Once you have that relationship with *you*, you get the gift of having it with another. With the awareness available to guide and help the inner child heal, outside events no longer trigger reactions based on old pain and old pain bodies.

Because the body holds the pain in its cellular memory, every emotional injury, assault, and trauma has a spot where it is held in the body. The body remembers, so we react from the feeling of the pain within the body. But, when we are *not* conscious, we actually ignore the feeling that the body is storing and react from the hurt inner child, from the emotion that is the expression of the pain. If we are in lack or fear, we may react with anger. If we are in shame, we may react with avoidance or disappointment. You see, the inner child is actually quite wise in the ways of how to protect the self. This is because it learned it coping skills long ago—or maybe not so long ago—and it acts out of self-protection. It does not want to be hurt again. It knows that pain, and it "tantrums" in order not to go back. It may also react by withdrawing, hiding, or not allowing themselves to be seen. It may present through becoming very quiet or still, or maybe hiding behind pounds of extra weight. But the result is the same. The true self cannot emerge, the injured self stays injured, and the false self stays in charge. It's a pattern and cycle that must be broken in order to heal and live, as Brene Brown calls it, a wholehearted life.

I believe that we all hold within us our own power and ability to heal. We all came to this physical form as pure, uninjured, whole energy, but based on the events of life, the events that each and every person has to face, a protective shield of the false self develops. On a cellular level, we all remember being whole; being enough; being worthy, important, loved, valued, light, joy, and abundant. We simply need to be brave enough to look inside, and that means we must look at the pain precisely where we have stored it.

When, through hypnosis, the inner child can have its voice heard by telling its story; release the pain; and receive healing and love from the adult loving self, the old files of beliefs and conclusions about the story can be removed from the cellular memory of the physical body and then the inner child can be shown a new, healthier way to cope and look at the story, and new coping skills can be put into place.

Once this happens, when old triggers are faced, they are no longer experienced in the same way and cannot be dealt with from the old perspective because that perspective has been shifted, re-parented, and healed. One can then be radiant, expansive, and limitless. This can lead to increased confidence, increased feelings of calmness, increased sense of self, increased feelings of being secure within the self, a decrease in anxiety, an improvement in mood, and an increase in the ability to trust in the self and take care of the self. The true self is allowed to be seen and heard more and more often without hesitation. You know and feel in your heart that you are worthy, you are enough, and you are indeed loved.

I have two more case studies I'd like to share with you to illustrate how transformative and healing this process is.

274 • JANET PHILBIN

Allison is a fifty-eight-year-old woman who was referred by her therapist for hypnotherapy due to severe
anxiety, which was impacting all areas of her life. Allison is
a healthcare professional working in an outpatient mental
health treatment program. Professionally, she understood
anxiety and knew she needed to find a way to feel better,
as it was beginning to impact not only her home life but
also her work.

Allison is also a two-time breast cancer survivor. She
had been in traditional talk therapy for a number of years
and knew she needed to do another type of therapy; the
talk therapy was only getting her so far. During the first
session, I took a detailed history and began to understand
that Allison was dealing with feelings of panic, fear, anger,
grief, and holding onto a lot of self-blame.

We got to work immediately, as Allison was very motivated. The first issue she chose to deal with was the emotion around her cancer diagnosis. Through hypnosis, we
went back to the day she got the first phone call, eleven
years earlier, when her doctor told her she had breast
cancer. In her mind's eye, she was able to see herself on
the bathroom floor feeling panic, confusion, and fear. It
was at this time that uncertainty took over. I guided her to
tune into her body and determine where these big feelings
were in terms of her chakras. She was able to identify
where she'd been holding them all these years and understand the thoughts and beliefs she developed that day and
held onto going forward. Her worst fear came true when,

after all the treatment and surgery, the cancer came back and she had to deal with it all over again.

Through the process of transformative hypnosis, she was able to find compassion and give understanding to her younger self for the development of her panic and anxiety. Healing this aspect of panic and fear related to her health enabled her to go back even further into her history. In another session, we were able to go back to a time when Allison was four years old. She saw her four-year-old self wanting to hug her mother to say goodnight. Her mother turned away from her. This hurt Allison deeply, and she held that pain deep in her spleen chakra, which made sense, as this is where our unexpressed emotional pain is stored. At that time, she made big decisions about herself, the most significant being that she did not need anybody and was not good enough. Again, through the healing process, we were able to work with her four-year-old self and help her to see the truth of the situation and understand that she made decisions at that time in order to survive. Gaining this understanding allowed adult Allison the freedom to find compassion and forgiveness for her four-year-old self.

At this point, we were able to start her healing and put new, healthy coping skills in place for her to use in her life going forward. In doing this, we let that little girl have the freedom to play, to no longer be responsible, to know she is loved and enough.

Finally, our big breakthrough came during a session when Allison was able to go back to a time of the limiting belief that said, "If I start to enjoy life, it will get taken away." Once again, we went back in time. This time, she was in her late twenties and had given birth to her first child. She was scared and anxious about having a baby who was totally dependent on her. I asked her to tune into her chakras, and she found that this worry was being held in her heart. It was so heavy with worry that she was finding it hard to breathe. She began to believe, at that time, that she had to take care of self and had no control, that she had to depend on her husband. She began to feel anxious. As we looked into how it was affecting her in the present, she realized that she is always trying to find a way out and making plans about how she will "make it." This developed into her beliefs about not being a good mother, which left her feeling angry and not good enough within herself. By the end of this session, through the healing process, she was able to let go of the anger; feel very calm; and feel good, worth it, loved, and peaceful.

We had a few more sessions, and with each one Allison reported a continued decrease in her anxiety. With this decrease in anxiety, she was no longer having panic attacks, and when her anxiety did come up, she was able to use the tools she had learned during the sessions with me to bring herself back into a place of balance. She left the last session feeling calm, healthy, healed, and joyful. That was one year ago. I have not heard from Allison since, and I hope she is continuing to live a balanced, calm, and healthy life.

Samantha came to me when she was twenty-two years old. She had an emotionally and sexually abusive childhood. Both parents also had a history of drug abuse. To say that Samantha had a traumatic childhood would be an understatement.

From her very first session, I was very impressed with Samantha, as she was motivated to do this hard work at a deep level because she knew she wanted more from her life than what she was currently experiencing. She had not finished college and was working as a head cashier at a large store. She often dissociated, and she felt numb all of the time. I worked with Samantha for over three years. Almost every session involved deep work using hypnosis, tapping into her chakras, and helping her to learn to stay present in her being state. We had to work on issues of self-worth, disempowerment, fear, boundaries, current relationships with men, feeling safe within herself, helping her stop her self-harming behaviors, post-traumatic stress, and shame.

Samantha never ceased to amaze me. During the course of our time working together, she began to experience the layers of healing. Some of those layers were very hard and painful to peel off, while others weren't as deep. With each layer we peeled off, Samantha healed. Slowly but surely, she began to make healthy decisions for herself, like ending bad relationships, establishing very firm boundaries with her parents, and beginning classes again at a community college. She eventually got a new office job with benefits and a higher salary. She began to believe in herself and know her self-worth, and she was no longer engaging in self-harming behaviors. If she got triggered, she would still go numb and dissociate, but she recognized it as it happened and was able to use her new ability to stay present to bring herself back to the current moment. This led to her dissociative moments being less frequent and much shorter in duration.

By the end of our three plus years together, Samantha was different person. She had been accepted into a bachelor's degree program which would lead right into the master's degree she wanted in the career she always dreamed of pursuing. She was not in a relationship and was okay with being single. She was able to do all of this healing by committing to herself and not running away when it got too hard or too painful. She allowed herself to go through her pain and come out on the other side. It is possible that she may need therapy again in the future, and I know that when she is ready, she will seek that out.

Allow me to share with you what she told me at the end of our time working together.

"You have helped me to grow into a person I can be proud of. A few years ago, before I started talking to you, I don't believe I could have felt that way. When we first started talking and you told me it was possible to heal my stuff, I had no idea what that would feel like on the other side. You have given me the gift of self-worth through the healings and all the life lessons you helped guide me through. Thank you for believing in me before I ever could."

To sum it up, we work with the injured inner child to hear the story and understand how and why it drew the conclusions it made for and about itself. We then look at the conclusions the false self has identified with and help them understand that they are actually not those beliefs, that those beliefs were put in place only in order to cope and survive in those moments. Once the injured inner child agrees to let go of their responsibility in the story, they also agree to let go of the powerful emotions they have been holding onto for all these years. With this powerful shift, reframing can be implemented and new coping skills can be put in place as the self learns to be "true" to itself and hear the positive messages about itself. The adult self can integrate the new positive messages and know them to be valid in terms of who they are in the present. This allows one to move forward, bringing all of her gifts into the present moment with no—or a lot less—baggage attached. It is here that we find our healthy inner child once again.

Journal Prompts

- Look back at a time in your life that needs healing, allow yourself to get a picture of it.

- Ask yourself: Where in my body am I feeling uncomfortable? If I could draw a picture of the uncomfortable feeling, what would it look like? (give as many details as possible.)

- Have I felt this before? If yes, when? If no, why is it showing up now? If yes, why is it showing up again?

- Is there a part of me that knows this feeling?

- What is the story attached to this feeling?

- What did my younger self come to believe because of this story?

- Did the story create any patterns in my life that I am still impacted by today?

- Am I able to see why my younger self made up this story?

- Am I able to find compassion and forgive my younger self for the story?

- Let your younger self know that you, the adult, get it. You do not blame her. That you know she did the best she could do at that time with the resources she had available to her?

- Tell the younger one the truth about who you are now and where you are in your life now.

- Imagine sending your love out to your younger self, just like the love you send your child or loved one. Allow her to receive it. Let her know that the next time she feels upset, you will be there for her, that she is safe and survived.

CHAPTER 16

You Are Ready!

You made it to the end. Feel proud of yourself. I know how challenging this work is. It is much easier, in a way, not to do the work, but you have also learned that by not doing it, you suffer more. You have chosen you. You have chosen not to suffer. You have made a declaration to the universe that you are finished with your old ways and ready to take life on in a new way. You have opened yourself up to new ideas and are willing to look within.

Throughout this book, we have talked about healing—what it is and how to bring it into your life. I have broken it down, explained the chakras, and shared the Spiral of Healing with you. I have invited you to begin to meditate and journal. I have shared my journey and how/why hypnosis is so effective and helpful. When you learn to be aware of yourself and take care of your needs, you can be there for your children and others to support them, helping them be the person they came here to be without your own personal agenda getting in the way. In other words, you get to be. Remember the chart about "being" from the "Love" section of chapter 11. This is where and how being comes into play. Allowing yourself to be and allowing the other to be without expectation to be a certain way in order to feel better gives you emotional freedom. Expressing as someone other than who you truly are is expressing as the voice of your false self. As you heal yourself, you can help others in your life. It is as if healing your own heart gives others permission to heal their own. Healing starts with you.

Healing is transformative. This I promise you. If you let yourself take this journey and stick with it, you will get there. Be proud of yourself for getting this far. This work is not for the faint of heart. You are now able to recognize the voice in your head and can identify it as a lost part of yourself who is only looking for compassion, forgiveness, and love in order to feel better so it does not act out and knows it has the ability to heal. The transformative power of helping the inner child is enormous.

Through the journaling you have done as you journeyed through this book with me, you learned that *you* are your most powerful healer. You have the power and ability to help yourself in such a meaningful and life-changing way. You have the same ability to heal that resides inside each of us. Inside each of us is our whole, complete, true self. As you heal, you mend the holes left from childhood or other traumatic events. When you work from the inside out to heal these holes, you become whole once again.

Inside each of us is the light that we are. You are worth healing. You deserve to heal. Healing is possible.

Here is a final insight from one of my meditations for you to ponder as you continue on your path of your very own journey.

Experience the pure, untainted beauty of the now, because in the moment of the now is a sea of beauty that is meant to be experienced and then let go. And what happens when we let go? We are aware of the next moment of beauty, and that moment of beauty is no more or less beautiful than the moment before, it just is. We only have what is.

Remember, each moment is what it is. Pay attention to the way you show up in each moment. Allow yourself to see the beauty in each moment, as each moment has something to teach us. Being in the beauty of each moment allows you to be present, and in the present, there is no anxiety. What a beautiful place to be.

What happens now as you think about being in your open and loving heart? How will your life transform when you step into your heart space? I invite you to embrace your new being state.

In the beginning of the book, I asked you to look in the closet to find the young one who was hiding there. Have you fully taken that younger self out of the closet? Have you helped her find a level of healing and emotional freedom? What do you have to say to your younger self now? What does she have to say to you? You have reached the end, or maybe merely a new beginning. I am leaving you

290 • JANET PHILBIN

with one final journal prompt. As you answer these questions, think about the growth you have accomplished. Remember the one who was hiding and the way she has transformed. Place your hand on your heart, take a breath, close your eyes for a moment, and put your pen to the paper one last time with me.

Journal Prompts

- What were the things that kept you stuck?

- Did you release any belief systems? If so, which ones?

- What kind of shifts are you experiencing since releasing these belief systems?

- What new ideas do you have about your own ability to heal?

- Is it your day to blossom?

- Are you ready to bloom instead of staying stuck in the bud?

- What will change in your life when you put some of these principles into place?

Welcome aboard the Spiral of Healing. Enjoy the ride. You hold the ticket, so the power to get on and off the ride lies within you. I am honored you chose to take the ride with me. Remember, the most powerful one always available to help you during the ride is you.

Show up for yourself
On the breath, on the breath.
I am here, all shadow falls away.
My deepest truth is that I am all I need to be.
I am expansive,
I am abundant,
I am free and I am freedom,
I am fearless,
I am love,
I am really nothing but energy who has structure and form.
But that does not matter because form is an illusion.
When I can be the me that is my energetic self-
Then I walk in my truth!"

REFERENCES

Ban Breathnach, S. (1995). *Simple Abundance: A Daybook of Comfort and Joy.* New York, NY: Warner Books, Inc.

Brennan, B.A. (1987). *Hands of Light: A Guide to Healing Through the Human Energy Field.* New York, NY: Bantam Books.

Brown, B. (2012) *Daring Greatly: How the Courage to Be Vulnerable Transforms the Way We Live, Love, Parent, and Lead.* New York, NY: Penguin Random House.

Garrett, M.T. (1998) *Walking on the Wind: Cherokee Teachings for Harmony and Balance. Rochester, VT: Inner Traditions International.*

Krasner, A.M. (1990/1991) *The Wizard Within: The Krasner method of Hypnotherapy.* Irvine, CA: American Board of Hypnotherapy Press.

Singer, M.A. (2007). *The Untethered Soul: The Journey Beyond Yourself. Oakland, CA: New Harbinger Publications/Noetic Books.*

Tolle, E. (2005) *A New Earth: Awakening to Your Life's Purpose.* New York, NY: The Penguin Group.

Tsabary, S (2016) *The Awakened Family: A Revolution in Parenting.* New York, NY: Penguin Random House LLC.

ABOUT THE AUTHOR

Janet Philbin is a Licensed Clinical Social Worker with twenty-eight years of experience. She is a Certified Conscious Parenting Coach Practitioner, Certified Hypnotherapist, Certified Master An-Ra energy healer, and Certified Intuitive counselor. Janet is also a Hypnosynergistic® Therapy practitioner.

Janet studied with Dr. Shefali Tsabary and completed her training in Dr. Shefali's Conscious Parenting Coaching Method Institute. She has been teaching Conscious Parenting workshops since 2017.

She is passionate about teaching and helping parents awaken to help them develop strong connections with their children and themselves. Her goal is for parents to be able to honor the spirit and essence of their children.

www.JanetPhilbin.com

Made in the USA
Las Vegas, NV
15 February 2021